AMERICA AT RISK

‖‖ ‖ ‖‖‖‖‖‖‖‖ ‖ ‖‖‖‖ ‖ ‖‖ ‖‖‖‖‖‖‖‖ ‖‖‖
W9-CYB-794

THE CITIZEN'S GUIDE TO MISSILE DEFENSE

by James H.
Anderson, Ph.D.

The Heritage Foundation

The Heritage Foundation
214 Massachusetts Avenue, N.E.
Washington, D.C. 20002-4999
(202) 546-4400
http://www.heritage.org

On the cover: A modified U.S. Minuteman II missile rockets skyward from its silo at Vandenburg Air Force Base, California, on June 23, 1997. At the end of its trajectory, the missile delivered nine targets—including an unarmed reentry vehicle and various decoys—to a point on the ocean 4,300 miles downrange. Photo courtesy of Ballistic Missile Defense Organization, U.S. Department of Defense.

CONTENTS

FOREWORD

America today has no defense against ballistic missiles tipped with nuclear bombs, biological agents, or chemical gases. This may be difficult to believe, but consider this: Our vulnerability did not come about by accident. In fact, the only reason we are vulnerable today is deliberate policy decisions that date back to the Cold War, when the single greatest threat of missile attack came from our enemy, the Soviet Union.

The world is a very different place today. Our enemies are well aware of our vulnerability. States like Iran and North Korea, under erratic leaders, are developing long-range missiles and nuclear bombs. And last August, North Korea launched a three-stage rocket over Japan, proving that, despite our best efforts, weapons of mass destruction are proliferating more rapidly than our "experts" had imagined possible. States like Iraq hope to follow the same script, and eventually may try to exploit our nakedness to missile attack.

This should not be so. The technologies for deploying defensive systems to intercept hostile missiles have advanced dramatically in recent years. Yet, until now, the Clinton

Administration has refused to commit our resources to building an effective missile defense system to protect our families, our children, and our country from annihilation. The Administration remains wedded to a doctrine embodied in a treaty we signed in 1972 with a country that no longer exists. The Anti-Ballistic Missile (ABM) Treaty, more than anything else, prevented us from deploying missile defense systems during the Cold War. And it continues to do so today, because President Bill Clinton believes this treaty is still in force, even though America's only partner in the treaty, the Soviet Union, dissolved in 1991.

Unfortunately, America will remain at risk—and without an effective missile defense—so long as the Administration abides by this defunct agreement. The time has come for Americans to demand that the federal government fulfill its primary constitutional duty *to provide for the common defense.*

I am grateful to James H. Anderson, Ph.D., Defense and National Security Policy Analyst in The Kathryn and Shelby Cullom Davis International Studies Center at The Heritage Foundation, for writing this *Citizen's Guide to Missile Defense.* His lucid account details the ways in which the spread of ballistic missiles threatens every American, whether here at home or on duty overseas.

His analysis will fill an important niche in the growing public debate over the most affordable and effective means to deploy a national missile defense system. Unfortunately, this debate has been focused "inside the Beltway" for far too long.

Readers will need no technological expertise or background knowledge in national security to benefit from this discussion. In plain English, this book examines the strategic, legal, and moral dimensions of missile defense. Its analysis, without relying on confusing jargon or bewildering acronyms, details the threat from Third World rogue regimes and the very real danger of accidental and unauthorized missile launches from Russia or China.

It explains the reasons that the Clinton Administration's plan to deploy ground-based defenses will be inadequate to protect the country from these threats, and why a sea- and space-based approach would provide the most effective and affordable alternative.

Now, as was always the case, the health and survival of our republic depends on an informed citizenry—especially concerning issues of national security. *America at Risk: The Citizen's Guide to Missile Defense* is a vital contribution to the lexicon of freedom, sovereignty, and national security.

I hope you will encourage your friends, family members, and co-workers to read

America at Risk and join their voices with those who demand that our government provide for the "common defense" of America.

Edwin J. Feulner, Ph.D.
President
The Heritage Foundation
April 1999

PREFACE

> *Is it not time to awake from the deceitful dream of a golden age and to adopt as a practical maxim for the direction of our political conduct that we, as well as the other inhabitants of the globe, are yet remote from the happy empire of perfect wisdom and perfect virtue?*
> — Alexander Hamilton,
> *Federalist Papers* No. 6

A s Alexander Hamilton suggested many years ago, it is human nature to presume that relations among states inevitably will evolve along cordial lines. History, however, suggests otherwise. In the aftermath of the Soviet Union's sudden collapse in 1991, many Western leaders believed a "golden age" of peace and prosperity would replace Cold War-era tensions. This hope proved to be a false dawn. The Cold War's passage has left behind a more unpredictable, unstable, and, in some ways, even more dangerous world. Yet many Americans remain far too complacent about our national security.

Today, we need protection against a full range of threats, from terrorists operating on American soil to rogue states developing long-range missiles that they hope to arm with nuclear bombs, biological agents, or poisonous gas. We desperately need a "defense-in-depth" against myriad foreign dangers.

When you leave your home for vacation, you would not lock the doors but leave the windows open, or vice versa. Either scenario would make your home a lucrative target for intruders. The same logic applies to national security: Different threats require different actions. Thanks to such law enforcement agencies as the Federal Bureau of Investigation, we have some defenses against international terrorists who hope to wreak havoc on American soil. But we have *no* protection against ballistic missiles, whether launched deliberately or accidentally.

Most Americans find this vulnerability difficult to imagine; many believe our armed forces can shoot down any missile, anywhere, whenever we want. This common misperception is understandable. We are, after all, the wealthiest and most technologically advanced power in human history.

Alexander Hamilton's warning in the *Federalist Papers* is prescient. We need to "awake from the deceitful dream of a golden age" and get serious about protecting our vital political, economic, and military interests around the world. We must defend against many dangers, from terrorists and international criminals to rogue regimes that are capable of conventional aggression. Certainly, all these threats require vigilance. But protecting U.S. citizens against hostile missile attacks is a question of national survival. Nothing else will matter if we do not convince our elected representatives in Washington, D.C., to take prudent steps to ensure the safety of all Americans from this growing menace.

I wish to thank my coworkers in The Heritage Foundation's Kathryn and Shelby Cullom Davis International Studies Center for their many helpful suggestions. Most especially, I thank Kim R. Holmes, Ph.D., Vice President; Thomas Moore, Director; Baker Spring, Senior Policy Analyst; Jack Spencer, Research Assistant, for his indefatigable fact-checking; Chris A. Dobrota, Intern; Janice A. Smith, Managing Editor; and Richard Odermatt, Senior Editor. Finally, I thank Ann Klucsarits, Director; James V. Rutherford, Editing and Publishing Associate; and Thomas J. Timmons, Manager of Graphic Design Services of the Publishing Services Department. The dedication of these people helped to bring this book to fruition.

James H. Anderson, Ph.D.
Defense Policy Analyst
April 1999

INTRODUCTION

In June 2000, North Korea launches a sneak attack into South Korea that soon brings Seoul to the brink of declaring defeat. Seemingly an eerie replay of the Korean War in 1950, the United States rushes reinforcements to the peninsula in a desperate attempt to help save South Korea. After a bloody campaign, U.S. forces succeed in pushing North Korea's army back across the 38th parallel. This time, however, there is a horribly different ending.

As South Korean and U.S. forces drive north, Pyongyang fires three nuclear-tipped Taepo Dong-2 missiles at the United States. One splashes harmlessly into the Pacific Ocean, but the others strike San Francisco and Los Angeles. In a flash, America suffers more than 1 million casualties— the greatest single loss of life in its history. Radioactive fallout cuts a deadly swath across the country, contaminating crops and water supplies. Fears of additional missile attacks prompt a nationwide panic; looting and rioting erupt in major cities. The stock market crashes, wiping out billions of dollars of savings.

The President of the United States, under pressure to retaliate and prevent additional strikes from North Korea, unleashes a nuclear reprisal. The strike on Pyongyang kills over a million civilians and leaves the city a smoldering ruin.

*The President's decision helps to satisfy the desire
for revenge, but the nuclear retaliation inflames
anti-American sentiments throughout much of
Asia.*

*The turmoil in the United States forces the
President first to declare a national emergency and
shortly thereafter to declare martial law,
suspending civil and political freedoms in a
desperate bid to restore order. U.S. military forces
stationed overseas are rushed home to assist the
National Guard. Third World adversaries pounce
to exploit the crisis. Iraq invades Kuwait and
Saudi Arabia, and Iran closes off the Strait of
Hormuz. Allies openly question America's ability
to lead. And the chaos throws the international
economy into a tailspin.*

*Here at home, federal, state, and local officials
struggle to re-establish some semblance of order.
People wonder whether they ever will regain their
constitutional freedoms, and whether America ever
will reclaim its superpower status. Yet, amid all
the confusion, one thing is certain: North Korea's
devastating missile attacks on Los Angeles and
San Francisco will scar America for generations to
come.*

An impossible scenario? Far-fetched?
Unfortunately, the answer is "no."
Today, North Korea is led by an
unstable regime that makes no secret of its
longstanding desire to reunify the peninsula.
In August 1998, North Korea tested the Taepo

Dong-1, a three-stage rocket that some experts believe can reach parts of Hawaii and Alaska. North Korea is working feverishly on building the next-generation ballistic missile, the Taepo Dong-2, an even longer-range missile that is capable of reaching America's West Coast. Yet, despite this clear and present danger, and the fact that several other rogue states are seeking similar capabilities, the U.S. military lacks any means to intercept hostile missiles launched at American soil.

Like a malignant cancer, this threat has been growing for many years, ever since the Nazis launched V-2 missiles over the English Channel during the latter stages of World War II. Adolf Hitler's "vengeance weapons" were crude, short-range missiles designed to inflict maximum psychological terror. The missile threat is much broader today, and more lethal; nearly two dozen states are building ballistic missiles. Ominously, some of these states are seeking to marry these missiles with warheads containing nuclear bombs, biological agents, and poisonous gases. And the technology required to build these weapons has spread to many states. In 1998, for example, India and Pakistan became the latest states to join the nuclear club.

Ballistic missiles are capable of destroying life and property on a massive scale. Remember the horrific terrorist attacks on the World Trade Center in New York and

Oklahoma City's federal building? A missile armed with even a small nuclear warhead would unleash an explosion thousands of times more powerful than both of these blasts combined. Yet our country remains naked to these missiles. Every citizen needs to understand the reason we are in this predicament.

Learning more about missile defense may seem like a daunting task, especially because the technology appears so complex and the terminology so foreign. Opponents of national missile defense would have you believe the fundamental principles of missile defense are difficult to grasp. But they are mistaken. The experts have no monopoly on common sense. Self-defense and self-preservation are intuitive concepts, easy to understand.

President Ronald Reagan generated an intense public debate when he announced the Strategic Defense Initiative (SDI) in 1983. He hoped to focus America's technological prowess on building a national missile defense system. After President Reagan left office, however, our vulnerability to hostile missiles attracted only drips and drabs of media attention. Until recently, missile discussions were confined to a small circle of defense experts. The time is ripe for a much broader national debate regarding the best means of protecting our country against enemy missiles.

Every American has a personal stake in our national security. Although the missile threat may appear more abstract than, say, crime in your neighborhood, it is no less real or less deadly. That is because impoverished, unpredictable states like North Korea are developing missiles capable of striking American soil in less time than it takes to watch the evening news. If this were not frightening enough, we also remain exposed to accidental or unauthorized launches from Russia or China, which already have amassed arsenals of deadly missiles. *In effect, every American already is a hostage to the threat of missile attack, whether it is deliberate, unauthorized, or accidental.*

RESPONDING TO THE PROLIFERATION DANGER

The threat posed by ballistic missiles may seem overwhelming, but there is no reason to despair. Americans have surmounted fearsome challenges in the past, such as winning independence from a colonial oppressor, surviving a bloody Civil War, defeating fascist and communist aggressors bent on global conquest, enduring the Great Depression, and putting men on the moon. In overcoming these challenges, Americans demonstrated unparalleled courage and foresight. We need to summon these virtues again to protect our country against the scourge of ballistic missile proliferation.

Astonishingly, recent surveys indicate that many Americans believe we already are protected against long-range missiles.[1] The Clinton Administration has done little to remedy this misperception. Even worse, it seems to presume that the lack of public outrage over our vulnerability reflects general support for deferring the decision to build a national missile defense until June 2000.[2] Yet the threat posed by the proliferation of missiles to Third World countries is seeping into the public's consciousness, albeit slowly, as each passing month seems to bring unwelcome news that another rogue state has test-fired a new and longer-range missile. In January 1999, the Clinton Administration finally admitted the dangers of missile proliferation. "We're affirming there is a threat and the threat is growing," said Secretary of Defense William Cohen.[3]

National missile defense is likely to be a key issue in the 2000 presidential election. The President of the United States is, after all, the commander in chief of the armed forces and ultimately responsible for our national security. Regardless of what happens in the next election, however, this much is certain: The threat of missile attack will demand our attention so long as we remain unprotected.

This book is intended to educate Americans about this threat. It is written for the average citizen. It does not presume its readers are familiar with the threat, military technology, global events, or national security. It does not matter whether you live in Alaska, Maine, or somewhere in between; whether you are a teenager, single parent, soccer mom, or senior citizen; whether you are a Democrat, Republican, or Independent. *This book is written for every American because everyone deserves the best possible protection against the threat of ballistic missile attack.*

NOTES

[1]   The Center for Security Policy, *National Survey of Registered Voters*, July 26-29, 1998.

[2]   "This substantial investment includes funding for NMD deployment and underscores the Administration's commitment to NMD. However, no deployment decision has been made. A decision about deployment is planned for June 2000." Written statement of Secretary of Defense William S. Cohen before the Senate Armed Services Committee, February 3, 1999, p. 8.

[3]   U.S. Secretary of Defense William S. Cohen, Department of Defense Briefing, Washington, D.C., January 20, 1999.

1

NOWHERE TO HIDE: WHY EVERY AMERICAN IS VULNERABLE TO MISSILE ATTACK

It is not an accident that there are some 25 or 30 countries that have or are seeking and developing ballistic missiles. They are attractive. They are cheap. They can be launched from land and sea. They are versatile in the sense that they can carry chemical, biological, or nuclear warheads.

— Former Secretary
of Defense Donald
Rumsfeld, 1998[1]

America is at risk. On August 31, 1998, North Korea flight-tested a long-range missile over Japan, thereby demonstrating its potential to strike Alaska or Hawaii in the near future.[2] As former Secretary of Defense Donald Rumsfeld pointed out in 1998, the proliferation of ballistic missiles is a far more dangerous threat than most Americans realize.

It is true that, unlike many countries today, we no longer have to worry about hostile powers invading our land. The Atlantic and Pacific Oceans and our friendly

Map 1.1

Ballistic Missile Proliferation

Countries Possessing Ballistic Missiles

Afghanistan	China	Hungary	North Korea	Russia	Ukraine
Algeria	Croatia	India	South Korea	Saudi Arabia	U.A.E.
Argentina	Czech Republic	Iran	Libya	Slovakia	U.K.
Azerbaijan	Egypt	Iraq	Pakistan	South Africa	U.S.
Belarus	France	Israel	Poland	Syria	Vietnam
Bulgaria	Georgia	Kazakhstan	Romania	Taiwan	Yemen

Source: Center for Defense and International Security Studies, 1996.

neighbors in Mexico and Canada help to protect us from that particular danger. But our complacency about the threat of missile attack—against which today we are powerless to defend—is troubling.

To be sure, most Americans are aware that Russia and China have missiles capable of destroying American cities. Yet many remain unaware that more than two-dozen Third World countries are working feverishly to develop similar capabilities. Because these missiles need not be very accurate to cause catastrophic damage, they appeal to tyrants who seek to threaten millions of Americans from afar.

Map 1.2

Known or Probable Biological and Chemical Programs

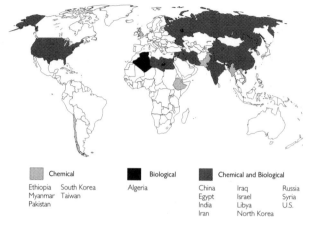

Chemical	Biological	Chemical and Biological		
Ethiopia South Korea	Algeria	China	Iraq	Russia
Myanmar Taiwan		Egypt	Israel	Syria
Pakistan		India	Libya	U.S.
		Iran	North Korea	

Source: Center for Non-Proliferation Studies, Monterey Institue of International Studies, 1999.

The threat of a ballistic missile attack on America, as Secretary of Defense William Cohen announced in January 1999, "is growing, and we expect it will soon pose a danger not only to our troop overseas but also to Americans here at home." This book will help you to understand this deadly peril and what we must do to protect our lives, families, and communities before it is too late.

THE COST OF DESTRUCTION

It is disturbing to imagine what would happen if an enemy missile landed on American soil—in New York, Philadelphia,

Map 1.3

Nuclear Proliferation

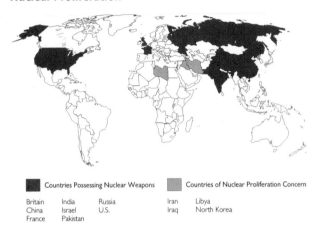

Countries Possessing Nuclear Weapons   Countries of Nuclear Proliferation Concern

Britain	India	Russia	Iran	Libya
China	Israel	U.S.	Iraq	North Korea
France	Pakistan			

Source: The Arms Control Association, *Fact Sheet,* "The State of Nuclear Proliferation," May 1998.

San Francisco, or Washington—especially if it carried a nuclear weapon. But this danger must be fully appreciated because no other threat has the potential to destroy, in the blink of an eye, lives and property on such a massive scale.

Seventy-five percent of all Americans live in urban areas, according to the most recent census.[3] Sprawling urban metropolises present large and inviting targets to those that would wish us harm. Los Angeles, for example, covers nearly 500 square miles.[4] But city residents are not the only citizens in danger. You and your family are at risk whether you reside in rural Maine, the plains of Kansas, the forests of Oregon, or any place in between.

Imagine if a nuclear-tipped missile struck a major West Coast city, such as Los Angeles, San Francisco, or Seattle. *In a flash, the attack would be likely to inflict more damage than America has suffered in all its previous wars combined.* The destruction wrought by even a single enemy missile would have serious consequences:

- **Immediate casualties.** In August 1945, the atomic bombings of Hiroshima and Nagasaki caused approximately 130,000 and 60,000 deaths, respectively.[5] The Hiroshima blast released the equivalent of 15 thousand tons of TNT; the Nagasaki bomb, 21 thousand tons.[6] By contrast, today's nuclear weapons often are measured in megatons—or millions of tons of TNT. The lethal blast and the damage from a 1-megaton bomb would be catastrophic. A 1979 Office of Technology Assessment study estimates that, if two 1-megaton warheads were to strike Philadelphia, the explosion would kill more than 400,000 people.[7]
- **Radioactive fallout.** Fallout from a nuclear blast would drift from west to east, spreading radioactive debris over thousands of square miles because of the prevailing winds. The radioactive "footprint" of this blast would

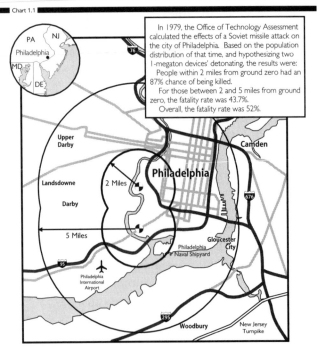

■ Chart 1.1 ■

PA NJ
Philadelphia
MD
DE

In 1979, the Office of Technology Assessment calculated the effects of a Soviet missile attack on the city of Philadelphia. Based on the population distribution of that time, and hypothesizing two 1-megaton devices' detonating, the results were:
People within 2 miles from ground zero had an 87% chance of being killed.
For those between 2 and 5 miles from ground zero, the fatality rate was 43.7%.
Overall, the fatality rate was 52%.

Upper Darby
Camden
Philadelphia
Landsdowne
2 Miles
Darby
5 Miles
Gloucester City
Philadelphia Naval Shipyard
Philadelphia International Airport
Woodbury
New Jersey Turnpike

A Two-Warhead Attack on Philadelphia: 410,000 Dead

Source: Office of Technology Assessment, *The Effects of Nuclear War,* 1979.

contaminate crops and water supplies across the country. Previous nuclear disasters have demonstrated the potential range of radioactive fallout and the harm it can inflict. In 1976, a Chinese nuclear test conducted halfway around the world produced radioactive fallout that landed on our East Coast.[8] The Chernobyl nuclear disaster in Russia in 1986 prompted a dramatic rise in the

Chart 1.2

Spread of the Radioactive Cloud Released from the Chernobyl Nuclear Power Plant, 1986

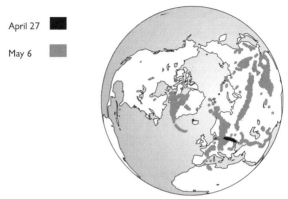

April 27

May 6

Source: Lawrence Livermore National Laboratory website, *http://air.llnl.gov/chernobl/source.html.*

incidence of thyroid cancer among children living near the accident and spread a radioactive footprint over thousands of miles.[9]

- **Economic fallout.** The costs of such an attack would be greater than any natural or manmade disaster America has suffered in the past. Take the destruction caused by Hurricane Hugo in 1989—that disaster cost more than $4 billion in insurance claims alone.[10] A nuclear weapon exploding over one of our major cities would inflict a far greater loss of life and property. The short-term medical and insurance costs alone would impose an onerous burden on Americans; the long-term reconstruction and decontamination costs would be staggering.

- **International fallout.** A successful missile strike on America would diminish our international influence. Rogue regimes in the Middle East, Asia, and elsewhere likely would be tempted to take advantage of our weakness and attack our overseas interests or those of our allies. For example, a dictator like Iraq's Saddam Hussein could exploit the crisis by attempting another land-grab in the Middle East. Allies would question the ability of the United States to continue to honor its security commitments overseas, considering such vulnerability at home.

- **Political and constitutional fallout.** Throughout American history, wars and economic crises have prompted a dramatic expansion of federal power and restrictions of our political and civil liberties. During the Civil War, for example, President Abraham Lincoln suspended the writ of *habeas corpus.* During the Great Depression, President Franklin Roosevelt dramatically increased the government's intervention in the economy. The Cold War witnessed an expansion of federal power as the Soviet threat forced America to create a vast national security bureaucracy[11] and maintain, for the first time in our history, a large standing army in peacetime. If the country suffered a missile attack, federal and state officials would be forced to take extraordinary measures to restore public order. The President would mobilize the National Guard and declare martial law, possibly for years. Many of the freedoms we take for granted would be subject to tight government control. Among other measures, the government would be likely to impose extensive press restrictions and curfews.

In sum, the loss of life and the physical, economic, and political fallout from a hostile missile strike would change our way of life for the worse and cast our future into doubt. In a word, the impact would be seismic. Clearly, the escalating proliferation of missiles, especially in the volatile Third World, should concern every American.

THE REASON MISSILES ARE SO POPULAR

After the Vietnam War, the U.S. military painstakingly restored its strength and integrity by instituting internal reforms. President Ronald Reagan's Administration deserves much of the credit for adequately funding the services and boosting military morale. Then, in 1991, our crushing defeat of Iraqi forces in Kuwait convinced many would-be aggressors that it would be foolish to challenge us on the battlefield. That is the good news.

Now the bad news: Hostile states seek desperately to offset our conventional prowess. Indeed, a former chief of staff of the Indian Army stated,

> The Gulf War emphasized once again that nuclear weapons are the ultimate coin of power. In the final analysis, they [the Americans] could go in because the United States had nuclear weapons and Iraq didn't.[12]

For Third World tyrants, missiles tipped with nuclear, biological, or chemical warheads offer several advantages over conventional explosives, including the potential to threaten millions of American civilians. Just imagine if Saddam Hussein rebuilt Iraq's ballistic missile program so that he could strike American cities.[13] Would anyone doubt that he would unleash such missiles in a crisis? Iraq, after all, fired Scud missiles at Israeli cities during the 1991 Persian Gulf War.

Third World dictators prefer missiles because they are less expensive to build and maintain than other delivery systems, such as long-range bombers or missile-carrying submarines. They also like these weapons

■ Table 1.1 ■■

Ballistic Missile Use in Regional Conflicts

	Date	Missile	Used by	Used Against
Yom Kippur War	1973	Scud	Egypt/Syria	Israel
		FROG	Egypt	Israel
Iran-Iraq War	1980–1988	Scud	Iraq/Iran	Iran/Iraq
		FROG	Iraq	Iran
U.S.-Libya	1986	Scud	Libya	Italy
Persian Gulf War	1991	Scud	Iraq	U.S. military forces,
		FROG	Iraq	Israel, Saudi Arabia,
				Qatar, Bahrain
Yemen Civil War	1994	Scud	Yemen	Yemen

Source: Ballistic Missile Defense Organization, *Fact Sheet,* DSI-98-01, "Ballistic Missiles and the World Security Environment," June 1998.

because they can exercise tight operational control over them. A tyrant armed with long-range missiles could threaten other countries without worrying about whether one of his bomber pilots might decide to defect.

The Missile Threat from Rogue Regimes

Today, we know that more than 20 states possess ballistic missiles or cruise missiles.[14] Many of these are lawless, rogue regimes that flagrantly disregard international norms of behavior by stoking the flames of disorder and supporting international terrorism. Such states include Cuba, Iran, Iraq, Libya, North Korea, Sudan, and Syria.[15] Many of these countries also have robust ballistic missile programs, which give them the potential to harm not only their immediate neighbors, but also civilian populations located

Chart 1.3

North Korea's Medium- and Long-Range Ballistic Missiles

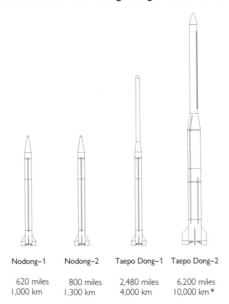

	Nodong–1	Nodong–2	Taepo Dong–1	Taepo Dong–2
Range	620 miles	800 miles	2,480 miles	6,200 miles
	1,000 km	1,300 km	4,000 km	10,000 km *

Note: * This estimate is for a lightweight variant. The Taepo Dong–2 has not yet been tested.
Sources: James Bruce, "South Korea Tables North's Ballistic Missile Sales," *Jane's Defence Weekly*, July 17, 1996; William Schneider, "Who Protects Japan?" *Defense News*, November 16-22, 1998; *Report of the Commission to Assess the Ballistic Missile Threat to the United States*, July 1998.

hundreds or even thousands of miles away.

Rogue states are hostile and unpredictable. During the Cold War, the Soviet Union behaved in a generally predictable, although adversarial, manner. Except for the Cuban Missile Crisis in October 1962, when the Soviets sought to sneak missiles into Cuba, they rarely took big risks. For the most part, China behaved cautiously as well. Both communist giants

Chart 1.4

North Korea's Potential Threat to America

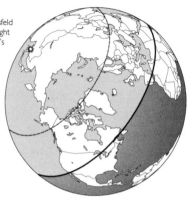

According to the Rumsfeld Commission, a lightweight variant of North Korea's Taepo Dong–2 missile would have a range of some 10,000 km (6,200 miles), putting a large portion of the United States at risk. The standard variant of the Taepo Dong–2 could have a range of up to 3,750 miles, capable of reaching Alaska and Hawaii.

Source: Range estimated based on *Report of the Commission to Assess the Ballistic Missile Threat to the United States*, July 1998.

knew that reckless behavior would increase the risk of conventional, perhaps even nuclear, war with the United States. For this reason, they preferred to sponsor indirect forms of aggression, including war-by-proxy, political subversion, and international terrorism.

Third World despots often behave less rationally than either the Soviet Union or China did during the Cold War. In 1991, for example, Saddam Hussein refused to withdraw his Iraqi forces from Kuwait despite being pummeled by coalition warplanes for six weeks. This megalomaniac is building multibillion-dollar palaces even as his people suffer from widespread malnutrition.

In North Korea, President Kim Jong-Il is spending billions of dollars to develop long-range ballistic missiles while thousands of his countrymen starve to death. Kim Jong-Il appears to live in a fantasy world. In 1983, he made a movie starring a Godzilla-like monster.[16] He reportedly ordered the kidnapping of two South Korean film stars to help North Korea to make better movies.[17] Kim Jong-Il also has a track record of terrorist activity. In 1987, he personally ordered the bombing of Korean Air Flight 858, which killed all 115 persons aboard.[18] His bizarre and dangerous behavior has direct implications for our safety.

The threat of retaliation may not be enough to dissuade leaders like Kim Jong-Il—who care little about human life—from launching ballistic missiles against Americans. For the threat of reprisal to deter aggression effectively, the opponent must be capable of making rational decisions. Herein lies the rub: It is unwise to presume, either today or in the future, that Third World leaders will act rationally.

Nobody knows exactly how much longer the rogue regimes in control of North Korea, Iraq, and Libya will endure. But if history is any guide, there always will be some rogues states among us. We can be virtually certain, moreover, that some of their leaders at times will act unpredictably, even irrationally.

THE RUMSFELD COMMISSION REPORT:
A WAKE-UP CALL

Until recently, the Clinton Administration downplayed the ballistic missile threat from the Third World. Its nonchalant attitude recently changed, thanks largely to a congressionally authorized assessment of this danger. In 1996, amid concerns that the Administration was soft-pedaling the threat of missile attack on the United States, Congress appointed a nine-member bipartisan commission of experts, chaired by former Secretary of Defense Donald Rumsfeld, to assess this threat. With access to classified intelligence data, they studied this menace in great detail.

> The loss of life and the physical, economic, and political fallout from a hostile missile strike would change our way of life for the worse and cast our future into doubt.

In July 1998, the Commission to Assess the Ballistic Missile Threat to the United States (the "Rumsfeld Commission") issued its eyebrow-raising report. The panel unanimously rejected a 1995 U.S. National Intelligence Estimate that we would face no direct ballistic missile threat before 2010.[19] The commission, in fact, found that the United States "might have little or no warning before operational deployment" of threatening ballistic missiles. The panel's key finding concluded that

> the threat to the U.S. posed by these emerging capabilities is broader, more mature and evolving more rapidly than has been reported in estimates and reports by the Intelligence Community.[20]

This alarming report provided Congress—and the American people—with a much-needed wake-up call about the growing threat of missile proliferation.

Despite the alarming findings of the Rumsfeld Commission's report and the Administration's belated admission that the threat is real and growing, President Bill Clinton still refuses to make a decision regarding the deployment of a national missile defense until 2000.

ACCIDENTAL OR UNAUTHORIZED MISSILE DANGERS

The missile threat posed by rogue leaders is not the only danger we face. Accidental missile launches could occur if a country mistakenly concluded it was under attack. This could result from human error, computer malfunction, or even some combination of these possibilities. Thinking its missiles might be destroyed on the ground, a country might conclude it is better to "use them or lose them."

In our country, nuclear weapons and ballistic missiles are subject to tight control. The military cannot launch missiles without the President's authorization. Yet not every country has a stable political system or a strong tradition of civilian control over the military. An unauthorized missile launch could occur if a rogue general or renegade political leader were to seize control of one (or more) of his country's ballistic missiles.

America faces dangers from both accidental and unauthorized missile launches. Russia and China, two nuclear powers with uncertain political futures, already have missiles capable of devastating our cities. Both these states are busy modernizing their arsenals of strategic missiles.[21] In fact, recent reports indicate Chinese espionage efforts have targeted our nuclear laboratories to steal highly sophisticated weapons designs.[22]

The deteriorating condition of Russia's military has attracted more attention, and for good reason. Almost a decade after the Cold War ended, Russia still possesses an estimated 22,000 nuclear weapons, along with over 700 tons of uranium and plutonium. In January 1999, U.S. Secretary of

Energy Bill Richardson asserted,

> The threat of Russian proliferation, Russian theft of nuclear weapons and scientists, of materials...is the most alarming threat that America has today.[23]

Several hair-raising incidents and disturbing trends have raised questions about Russia's control over its nuclear arsenal and illustrate the risk of accidental launch:

- In February 1999, news reports indicated that Russia's inability to replace monitoring satellites severely undermines its early warning system against missile attack.[24] In a crisis, then, Russian leaders would lack the ability to assess accurately the status of U.S. nuclear forces or those of any other nuclear power, thus increasing the risk of launch error.

- In September 1998, a Russian sailor assigned to the nuclear submarine *Bars* (Snow Leopard) ran amok and killed eight fellow crew members before committing suicide. The *Bars* normally is equipped to carry nuclear-tipped cruise missiles.[25]

- In September 1998, Russian workers went on strike at the Russian Federal Nuclear Center (formerly known as Chelyabinsk–70) and the Research Institute of Experimental Physics (formerly known as Arzamas–16), two nuclear weapons-producing cities. Some workers in Russia's nuclear industry had not been paid for five months.[26]

- In January 1995, Russia misidentified a Norwegian weather rocket to be a U.S. missile. The incident reportedly led President Boris Yeltsin to believe we had unleashed a preemptive attack on his country.[27]
- In August 1991, President Mikhail S. Gorbachev reportedly lost control of Russia's nuclear arsenal during a failed coup attempt.[28]

Concerned over the threat of "loose nukes" in the former Soviet Union, Congress has backed efforts to help to reduce this danger. The Nunn-Lugar Cooperative Threat Reduction Program, from legislation sponsored by Senators Sam Nunn (D-GA) and Richard Lugar (R-IN), has appropriated nearly $3 billion since 1991 to assist former Soviet states in dismantling their weapons of mass destruction and reducing the threat of proliferation. Can we be assured that Russia and China will take the necessary precautions to prevent accidental or unauthorized nuclear launches? The answer is "no."

Nuclear Mishaps

During the Cold War, the world came perilously close to accidental detonation on several occasions. For example, in January 1966, a B-52 bomber carrying four nuclear bombs crashed off the coast of Spain after colliding with a KC-135 tanker. Two years later, in January 1968, another B-52 carrying four nuclear weapons crashed near Thule Air Base in Greenland.[29] Although neither accident resulted in a nuclear detonation, both incidents spread radioactive debris over wide areas and required lengthy and costly cleanup operations. Many of these types of accidents, known as "broken arrows," remain shrouded in secrecy.[30]

Our country has decades of experience in handling nuclear weapons and materials. States that have recently joined the nuclear club, such as India and Pakistan, do not. The danger of accidental and unauthorized missile launch will increase as more countries develop these deadly weapons and the means to deliver them.

At any given moment, the threat of an accidental or unauthorized launch may appear slim. But taking a "snapshot" view of this risk is misleading. Over time, these dangers will increase as the number of states that develop nuclear weapons and ballistic missiles rises. For this reason, the decision to

Chart 1.5

Long-Range Ballistic Missiles Iraq Sought to Build

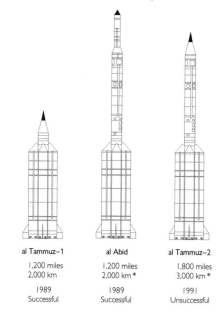

	al Tammuz–1	al Abid	al Tammuz–2
Range	1,200 miles 2,000 km	1,200 miles 2,000 km *	1,800 miles 3,000 km *
Tested	1989 Successful	1989 Successful	1991 Unsuccessful

Note: * Iraqi claim.
Sources: Lt. Gen. Daniel Graham, National Press Club Briefing, November 1, 1990; Bradley Burston, "Iraq: We Fired New Missile at Dimon," *The Jerusalem Post*, February 18, 1991; W. Seth Carus and Joseph Bermudez, Jr., "Iraq's Al-Husayn Missile Programme," *Jane's Intelligence Review*, June 1, 1990.

leave America defenseless in a world in which hostile states are armed with ballistic missiles is an unconscionable gamble.

We cannot know or dictate the future for Russia or China; nor can we ensure that other states will retain tight control over their nuclear arsenals. But there *is* something we can do. We can work to protect ourselves against catastrophic accidents by deploying defenses capable of protecting all Americans from deliberate, accidental, or unauthorized missile attack. Unfortunately, the Clinton Administration has said it will not make a decision to deploy such protection until 2000. And even if the President commits the country to build such defenses, they will not be ready until 2005 at the earliest.

PROSPERITY IS NOT ENOUGH

Our economic strength has lulled some Americans into a false sense of security. Yet our gross national product, impressive as it is, cannot stop a single incoming missile. Foreign leaders bent on destroying an American city will not be deterred by our material affluence. The fact that our cities remain unprotected has given Third World states like North Korea and Iran perverse incentive to accelerate their missile programs.

History teaches us that wealth alone is no guarantee against foreign aggression. We had a much larger gross domestic product than Japan prior to World War II, but that did not prevent Japan from attacking Pearl Harbor in December 1941. Iraq invaded oil-rich yet militarily weak Kuwait in 1990. The lesson is clear: *Affluent states that lack military preparedness invite aggression, not respect.*

Prudence dictates that we deploy a national missile defense before, not after, rogue states acquire missiles capable of destroying American cities. If you knew that a crime wave was headed toward your neighborhood, you would move quickly to improve the door and window locks of your home, or possibly move out of that neighborhood entirely. Unfortunately, the Clinton Administration has yet to show a similar sense of urgency regarding the missile threat.

We should *not* have to play catchup with rogue states that are developing missiles. The failure to deploy a national missile defense will allow unpredictable Third World despots to seize the political and military initiative. That outcome is a recipe for disaster.

NOTES

[1]   Donald H. Rumsfeld, Remarks before the Center for Security Policy's Ninth Annual "Keeper of the Flame" Award Dinner, October 7, 1998, Washington, D.C.

[2]   Dana Priest and Sandra Sugawara, "North Korea Missile Test Threatens Nuclear Pact," *The Washington Post*, September 1, 1998, p. A15.

[3]   U.S. Bureau of the Census, *1990 Census*, October 1995.

[4]   The Bureau of the Census cites 498.5 square miles. U.S. Bureau of the Census,

1990 CPH-2-6 Population and Housing Unit Counts, California, Table 9, p. 38.

5   Martin Sherwin, "Hiroshima and Nagasaki Bombings of 1945," *Encyclopedia of U.S. Foreign Relations* (New York, N.Y.: Oxford University Press, 1997), p. 296.

6   Stephen Schwartz, ed., *Atomic Audit: The Costs and Consequences of U.S. Nuclear Weapons Since 1940* (Washington, D.C.: Brookings Institution Press, 1998), p. 58.

7   Office of Technology Assessment, *The Effects of Nuclear War* (Washington, D.C.: U.S. Government Printing Office, 1979).

8   Anthony Robbins and Katherine Yih, *Radioactive Heaven and Earth* (New York, N.Y.: The Apex Press, 1991), p. 153.

9   See "Chernobyl Conference Sums Up Scientific Understanding," International Atomic Energy Agency *Newsbriefs,* Vol. 11, No. 2 (April/May 1996), p. 1.

10   *Wall Street Journal Almanac 1999* (New York, N.Y.: Ballantine Books, 1998), p. 637.

11   The 1947 National Security Act created the National Security Council, the Central Intelligence Agency, the Joint Chiefs of Staff, and the Air Force as a separate U.S. military service.

12   General K. Sundarji, quoted in Selig S. Harrison and Geoffrey Kemp, "India and America After the Cold War," Carnegie Endowment for International Peace, 1993, p. 20.

13   "Iraq has maintained the skills and industrial capabilities needed to reconstitute its long range ballistic missile program." See "Executive Summary," *Report of the Commission to Assess the Ballistic Missile Threat to the United States,* Published Pursuant to Public Law 201, 104th Congress, July 15, 1998, p. 14, hereinafter called the "Rumsfeld Commission Report."

14   William S. Cohen, *Annual Report to the President and the Congress* (Washington, D.C.: U.S. Government Printing Office, 1998), p. 63. See also Nonproliferation Center, *The Weapons Proliferation Threat,* U.S. Central Intelligence Agency, March 1995, p. 2.

15   The State Department lists these states as sponsors of international terrorism. See U.S. Department of State, *Patterns of Global Terrorism,* April 1998, p. iv.

16   James Hattori, *CBS This Morning,* October 19, 1994.

17   "Death of 'Great Leader' Raises Danger of Chaos at Critical Time," *The Cincinnati Enquirer,* July 9, 1994, p. A2.

18   See Eileen MacDonald, *Shoot the Women First* (New York, N.Y.: Random House, 1991), pp. 51, 53.

19   Baker Spring, "The Rumsfeld Commission Corrects a Faulty Assessment of the Missile Threat,"

Heritage Foundation *Executive Memorandum* No. 543, July 24, 1998.

[20] "Executive Summary," Rumsfeld Commission Report, p. 5.

[21] Russia has begun to deploy the SS-27 Topol-M intercontinental ballistic missile; China is working on the DF-31, a road-mobile missile with a range of 8,000 kilometers. See David Hoffman, "Russian Rocket Called Invincible," *The Washington Post,* February 25, 1999, p. A20; see also Paul Beaver, "China Prepares to Field New Missile," *Jane's Defence Weekly,* February 24, 1999, p. 3.

[22] Jim Mann, "U.S. Acquiesced in China Spying, Record Shows," *The Los Angeles Times,* March 14, 1999, p. 1.

[23] *60 Minutes II,* a CBS special report on "Krasnoyarsk-26," January 13, 1999.

[24] David Hoffman, "Russia's Missile Defenses Eroding; Gaps in Early-Warning Satellite Coverage Raise Risk of Launch Error," *The Washington Post,* February 10, 1999, p. A1.

[25] "Russian Draftee Commandeers Submarine, Is Killed by Troops," *Seattle Post-Intelligencer,* September 12, 1998, p. A2.

[26] Associated Press, "Russian Nuclear Workers Go on Strike," September 7, 1998.

27 See Peter Pry, *War Scare: Russia and the United States on the Nuclear Brink* (Westport, Conn.: Praeger, forthcoming 1999).

28 Celestine Bohlen, "Gorbachev Lost Control, Russians Report," *The New York Times*, August 23, 1992, p. 3.

29 The Brookings Institution, *U.S. Nuclear Weapons Cost Study Project*, 1998. Available at *http://www.brook.edu/fp/projects/nucwcost/box7-3.html*.

30 For a detailed look at accidents involving nuclear weapons, see Scott Sagan, *The Limits of Safety: Organizations, Accidents, and Nuclear Weapons* (Princeton, N.J.: Princeton University Press, 1995).

2

FALSE SENSE OF SECURITY: WASHINGTON'S MAD MENTALITY

Today, it makes no sense at all to grant Russia a veto over our capacity to defend ourselves. We should give notice and withdraw from the [ABM] treaty. Without a national and theater missile defense, we are without protection from weapons of mass destruction targeting our cities and blackmailing our policymakers and allies. No president has the right to ignore the common defense.

> — Former U.S. Representative to the United Nations Jeane Kirkpatrick, 1999[1]

How did America become so vulnerable to ballistic missiles? And why would our elected leaders leave us naked before the threat of missile attack? These core questions are being asked in coffee shops, living rooms, and schoolrooms today. It is difficult for anyone to comprehend the reason that, when America can put men on the moon and a robot on Mars, Washington has not deployed a protective shield to defend our country from hostile missile attack.

For many years, strategists considered the atomic bomb the absolute weapon. This was understandable; the bombings of Hiroshima and Nagasaki helped to prompt Japan's surrender in World War II. Strategists also once believed ballistic missiles were unstoppable, following Nazi Germany's use of V-2 rockets against Great Britain during that same conflict.

But technology seldom remains static. After World War II, scientists discovered that bombers and missiles used to deliver warheads might not be invincible after all. In the 1970s, the United States actually deployed some interceptors armed with nuclear warheads that were designed to destroy incoming missiles. Extremely primitive by today's technological standards, that system was intended to protect America from the emerging threat of Chinese ballistic missiles.

Before dismantling this limited system, the United States signed the Anti-Ballistic Missile (ABM) Treaty with the Soviet Union in 1972, which prevented us from developing a national system capable of protecting us from missile attack. Its advocates presumed this treaty would reduce the incentive to build additional offensive weapons, but this assumption turned out to be false. The Soviets kept building ever more deadly missiles, forcing the United States to deploy more advanced offensive systems. The treaty partners lived like two rattlesnakes in a barrel, each with the ability to kill the other but unable to escape deadly retaliation.

REAGAN'S STRATEGIC DEFENSE INITIATIVE

President Ronald Reagan was frustrated by this open-ended competition with the Soviet Union, which emphasized building ever more sophisticated nuclear weapons. He sought instead a long-term strategy that would reduce America's dependence on offensive weapons and retaliatory threats.

Toward this end, President Reagan announced the Strategic Defense Initiative (SDI) on March 23, 1983. He called

> upon the scientific community in our country, those who gave us nuclear weapons, to turn their great talents now to the cause of mankind and world peace, to give us the means of rendering these nuclear weapons impotent and obsolete.[2]

In short, President Reagan challenged the conventional wisdom that deterrence—the ability to dissuade aggression—was best served by preserving a suicide pact with the Soviet Union. He concluded that this posture, aptly known as *mutual assured destruction,* or MAD, was immoral and too costly.

Much has transpired since President Reagan articulated his vision more than 16 years ago. The technology to track and intercept hostile missiles has advanced dramatically. The Soviet Union disappeared in 1991, leaving Russia and 14 other independent states in its wake. Instead of facing the threats posed by one opponent and a massive nuclear exchange, America today is confronted with a nasty array of threats from many Third World countries that are accelerating their ballistic missile programs.

Sadly, one thing has not changed: American citizens remain naked to missile attack.

CLINTON'S CUTBACKS

In his January 1991 State of the Union address, President George Bush directed that the SDI be "refocused on providing protection from limited ballistic missile strikes—whatever their source."[3] His plan, the Global Protection Against Limited Strikes (GPALS) program, was appropriate because the primary threat no longer involved a massive attack from the Soviet Union. GPALS was designed to protect Americans from Third World ballistic missiles and accidental or unauthorized launches from either Russia or China. President Bush's plan called for GPALS deployment to begin in 1996.

President Bill Clinton canceled GPALS in 1993. He offered instead a "3+3" plan in 1995, in which three years of further research would precede any deployment decision; if the decision were made to deploy, then an additional three years would be needed to deploy a protective system. Since then, this timetable has slipped two additional years. Consequently, the Clinton Administration is not scheduled to make an initial *decision* to deploy until June 2000, nearly eight years after President Clinton took office. Even if the President eventually committed to building a national missile defense, his timetable would not call for deploying any protective system until 2005.

In January 1999, the Clinton Administration finally admitted "there is a threat and the threat is growing" with respect to missile proliferation. Yet its plan to cope with this threat lacks both urgency and focus. The Administration's fixation with arms control has prevented it from developing a cost-effective plan capable of protecting every American from missile attack.

THE ABM TREATY: AN ILLUSION OF SECURITY

An international treaty is a contract between two or more states. Following years of laborious negotiations, the United States signed the ABM Treaty, which forbade either treaty partner from deploying a nationwide system to intercept hostile missiles. Yet the Soviet Union repeatedly and intentionally has violated both the letter and spirit of this treaty.[4] Even former Soviet Foreign Minister Eduard Shevardnadze admits that Moscow cheated on its 1972 agreement with the United States.[5]

Today, we live in a radically different world. The Berlin Wall fell in 1989, creating a unified Germany. The Soviet Union dissolved in 1991, leaving behind Russia and 14 newly independent states. Yet the Clinton Administration believes the United States still is bound by the ABM Treaty. Arms Control and Disarmament Agency Director John Holum called it "one of the sacred texts of arms control."[6] In February 1999, Secretary of State Madeleine Albright referred to the ABM Treaty as a "cornerstone of our strategic stability."[7]

They are wrong. We are under no obligation to abide by treaties that undermine national security, or cleave to agreements that no longer bind the United States as a matter of international or constitutional law.[8] Numerous legal scholars and strategists have concluded that the ABM Treaty is legally dead.[9] Even Former Secretary of State Henry Kissinger no longer believes the ABM Treaty is binding. As recently as March 1999, Dr. Kissinger stated, "I wouldn't let it stand in the way" of missile defense.[10] Dr. Kissinger's view is important because the ABM Treaty was negotiated while he was National Security Adviser to the President.

The Soviet Union's dissolution is key to understanding the reason this agreement no longer is binding. Imagine if you signed a contract with world famous opera singer Luciano Pavarotti to sing at your wedding, but he was unable to perform because of an unexpected throat infection. You would not expect Mr. Pavarotti's lawyer, publicist, or vocal coach to sing in his place. The contract you signed was personal, based on the reasonable expectation that Mr. Pavarotti himself would provide the service.[11]

> Even if the President eventually committed to building a national missile defense, his timetable would not call for deploying any protective system until 2005.

Similarly, the ABM Treaty was linked inextricably with the Soviet Union's geographic and legal personality. U.S. and Soviet negotiators painstakingly drafted the treaty and a follow-on 1974 protocol after thousands of hours of haggling over the precise wording because the treaty defined a specific strategic relationship between the United States and the Soviet Union.

Nevertheless, the Clinton Administration seeks to alter the ABM Treaty to include Belarus, Kazakhstan, Russia, and Ukraine, and negotiated agreements to that effect with representatives of those countries in New York in 1997. This attempt is misguided because neither Russia nor any combination of the successor states is capable of fulfilling the Soviet Union's geographic or legal personality or the original purpose of the ABM Treaty. The attempt raises the international principle of law known as *impossibility of performance,* which means the original terms of the treaty cannot be fulfilled because no would-be successor state is capable of fulfilling them.

The Clinton Administration also believes it is possible to deploy a national missile defense that preserves the basic terms of the ABM Treaty. But any effort to build a robust anti-missile system under this agreement would prove futile, like trying to square a circle. Moreover, the Administration's plan to limit a defensive system for America to one or two fixed ground-based sites would lack the depth afforded by a sea-based and space-based system.[12] The Administration's plan would result in an ineffective defense system at a higher cost.[13]

THE MYTH OF STRATEGIC STABILITY

To defend their commitment to the ABM Treaty, Clinton Administration officials like Secretary Albright often invoke the mantra of strategic stability. In theory, this term describes circumstances in which the danger of missile attack is minimal. In reality, the Administration's concept of strategic stability has perpetuated our vulnerability to the growing threat of hostile missile attack. Preoccupation with the ABM Treaty for its own sake will not protect America from an accidental or unauthorized missile launches; nor will it dissuade a deranged leader from trying to kill thousands, perhaps even millions, of Americans.

Adhering to the ABM Treaty is unnecessary because it is legally dead; undesirable because it would be less effective than building defenses without those constraints; and unfair because it places no restrictions on those Third World states that are building long-range missiles.

The Clinton Administration's approach is both dangerous

and unfair. Why should we remain defenseless when other states are feverishly arming themselves with long-range weapons? No treaty prevents rogue states like Iran, Libya, and North Korea from developing ballistic missiles. Instead of a cornerstone of strategic stability, as President Clinton would have you believe, the ABM Treaty is a millstone around the necks of all Americans.

Every country has the right to self-defense. This internationally recognized principle finds expression in Article 51 of the United Nations Charter. Self-defense is not only a practical option; it is a moral imperative. Yet we in America remain naked to missile attack because our leaders have chosen vulnerability as a matter of national policy, not because of any constitutional or international legal restraint.

The ABM Treaty does not advance national security any more than the old Kellogg–Briand Pact that presumed to "outlaw" war in the 1920s. Germany and Japan shamelessly exploited the propaganda benefits of signing that pact to mask their evil intentions. They sensed other countries valued safety more than freedom. The Kellogg–Briand Pact, like the ABM Treaty today, lulled many well-meaning people into a false sense of security. Unfortunately, this attitude helped to convince Nazi Germany and Imperial Japan that civilized countries lacked the fortitude to defend themselves.

During the Cold War, ABM Treaty advocates believed it would end the offensive arms race. But the arms race continued, waning when President Reagan achieved substantive arms reductions in the 1980s—and only then after he introduced the SDI. ABM Treaty apologists continue to defend the treaty today, despite the clear and present danger posed by ballistic missile proliferation in Third World states.

Adhering to the ABM Treaty constraints is unnecessary because this treaty is legally dead; undesirable because it would be less effective than building defenses without those constraints; and unfair because it places no restrictions on those Third World states that are building long-range missiles. The ABM Treaty even impedes testing and development of anti-ballistic missile technologies that could intercept short-range missiles.[14] This hinders our ability to protect our troops overseas that are in harm's way.

In sum, it is neither smart nor fair to remain bound by the constraints of the ABM Treaty, a Cold War fossil that prevents America from protecting its citizens against the threat of missile attack. The 1972 ABM Treaty has become the Kellogg–Briand Pact of our time: irrelevant, outdated, and overtaken by events. The Clinton Administration's defense of the ABM Treaty sends the message to our adversaries that the United States is more concerned with preserving paper agreements than protecting its citizens. This is dangerous and wrong. We must deploy a robust national missile defense as soon as technologically feasible. President Clinton and Congress immediately should consign the ABM Treaty to where it belongs— the scrapyard of history.

NOTES

[1] Jeane J. Kirkpatrick, "Target America," *National Review,* February 22, 1999, p. 30.

[2] President Ronald Reagan, *Address to the Nation on National Security,* March 23, 1983.

[3] President George Bush, *State of the Union Address,* January 29, 1991.

[4] See "Appendix C: Soviet/Russian Violations of the ABM Treaty," in *Defending America: A Plan to Meet the Urgent Missile Threat,* Report by The Heritage Foundation's Commission on Missile Defense (Washington, D.C: The Heritage Foundation, 1999).

[5] "U.S. Praises Admissions by Shevardnadze," *The Washington Post,* October 25, 1989, p. A42.

[6] "I turn now to a growing menace that has led some people mistakenly to surmise that we are lessening our commitment to

one of the sacred texts of arms control—the Antiballistic Missile (or ABM) Treaty." John D. Holum, Director, U.S. Arms Control and Disarmament Agency, in an Address to the Center for National Security Negotiations, Wilton Park Conference, United Kingdom, April 1994.

[7] Secretary of State Madeleine Albright, Testimony Before the Foreign Relations Committee, U.S. Senate, 106th Cong., 1st Sess., February 24, 1999.

[8] David B. Rivkin, Jr., Lee A. Casey, and Darin R. Bartram, "The Collapse of the Soviet Union and the End of the 1972 Anti-Ballistic Missile Treaty: A Memorandum of Law," The Heritage Foundation, June 15, 1998. The Washington, D.C., law firm Feith & Zell released a legal memorandum on February 1, 1999, that reaches conclusions similar to those of this study.

[9] Rivkin et al., "The Collapse of the Soviet Union and the End of the 1972 Anti-Ballistic Missile Treaty."

[10] Henry Kissinger, in remarks at The Heritage Foundation Missile Defense Conference, Washington, D.C., March 23, 1999.

[11] The author thanks his Heritage Foundation colleague, Baker Spring, for this analogy.

12   See *Defending America: A Plan to Meet the Urgent Missile Threat.*

13   For a detailed cost estimate of the Clinton Administration's plan, see U.S. General Accounting Office, *National Missile Defense: Even with Increased Funding Technical Risks Are High*, Report to Congressional Requesters, GAO/NSIAD-98-153, June 1998.

14   Baker Spring, "The ABM Treaty—Not Political Pressure—Causes Risks in Missile Defense," Heritage Foundation *Executive Memorandum* No. 521, April 3, 1998.

3

ENDING THE IMMORALITY OF VULNERABILITY: THE CASE FOR MISSILE DEFENSE

Wouldn't it be better to save lives than to avenge them?
> — President Ronald Reagan, 1983[1]

In 1991, during the Persian Gulf War, the United States rushed Patriot missile batteries to Israel to help to protect Tel Aviv from missile attack. In April 1994, we sent Patriot missiles to South Korea to reassure that country during a period of high tension. In January 1999, we dispatched Patriots to Turkey when Iraq threatened missile attack. Congress also has allocated funds for upgrading defensive systems capable of protecting our troops and our allies against short-range ballistic missiles.

These actions were justified, but they raise a critical question: Is it fair to protect U.S. service personnel overseas and citizens of other countries from missile attack but leave the American people without any protection at home? The answer is "no." Leaving Americans vulnerable to ballistic missiles armed with nuclear, chemical, or biological weapons is immoral. As a matter of principle, American citizens should be afforded the same level of protection the government affords our troops and allies overseas.

AMERICA IS WORTH DEFENDING

Some opponents of a robust defensive system for the American homeland believe our country is morally no better than any other. This specious reasoning appears under many different guises. During the Cold War, for example, some commentators claimed that we were no better than the Soviet Union. Some even equated President Ronald Reagan's liberation of Grenada in 1983 with the Soviet invasion of Afghanistan in 1979. The inability of opponents to discern the moral difference between the use of force to liberate a captive people, as happened in Grenada, and the brutal oppression of an independent state, as in Afghanistan, reflects a willful bias against our country.

National security matters little to those who believe America is not worth protecting. The logical extension of this view is not merely opposition to missile defense, but an argument for total disarmament. After all, if America is not worth defending against missile attack, why bother to defend it against any other threat? But leaving America defenseless against foreign threats is not the answer. It is instead a shameful form of moral surrender.

The peace-through-disarmament approach has ended in disaster in the past. In 1933, students in Great Britain took the Oxford Union pledge not to "fight for King and country." For its part, the British government tried to appease Nazi Germany during the interwar period. Britain failed to appreciate the fearsome implications of Germany's rearmament.

Today, opponents of missile defense are making a similar mistake. No Third World country has the ability to conquer Europe and Asia, as the Nazis sought to do during World War II. But by building missiles capable of striking U.S. cities, they are developing a lethal capacity about which Adolf Hitler could only dream. Underestimating this danger is a prescription for disaster.

Is it fair to protect U.S. service personnel overseas and citizens of other countries from missile attack but leave the American people without any protection at home?

THE GOVERNMENT'S DUTY IS TO DEFEND

In introducing his Strategic Defense Initiative (SDI), President Reagan observed that the reliance on retaliation is a "sad commentary on the human condition."[2] He was right. The U.S. government has the constitutional duty to "provide for the common defense," as stated in the Preamble to the Constitution. This crucial phrase is repeated in Article I, Section 8, which also describes in detail Congress's responsibilities.

The government also has the moral duty to defend all Americans, regardless of where they live. To suggest otherwise would imply that citizens of some states somehow are more worthy than others, or that some states are more deserving. No American would agree with that implication. Yet, in 1995, the Clinton Administration did exactly that when it asked the intelligence community to conduct a threat assessment of the "contiguous 48 states and Canada." Consequently, the November 1995 National Intelligence Estimate did not include Alaska or Hawaii in that assessment.[3] Because of their geographic position, however, Alaska and Hawaii are the two states most vulnerable to missiles launched from North Korea.

At its core, protecting ourselves against missile attack is a sovereignty issue. Our country has a unique political and legal identity dedicated to life, liberty, and the pursuit of happiness. These values are worth protecting.

Yet those who believe the United Nations can defend American values and security interests would have us relinquish our national sovereignty to international institutions. The United Nations can play a constructive, if somewhat limited, role in mediating some foreign conflicts. But entrusting our national security to the United Nations, or any other international body, is a recipe for disaster. These organizations will not protect us from international terrorists, criminals, or missile attacks. Protecting American lives is the responsibility of our elected leaders in Washington.

America's Founding Fathers certainly believed the government has the clear duty to protect its citizens from foreign and domestic threats. They knew that no government that abdicated its solemn duty to protect its citizens would retain the loyalty of its citizens, the allegiance of its allies, or the respect of its foes. Unfortunately, the Clinton Administration's determination to preserve the defunct Anti-Ballistic Missile (ABM) Treaty has perpetuated its immoral policy of leaving our country naked to the threat of missile attack.

SELF-DEFENSE IS MORALLY SUPERIOR TO RETALIATION

The United States has adopted a nuclear posture that rests on two moral contradictions: First, the government's duty to "provide for the common defense" conflicts with its unwillingness, at least thus far, to provide the American people with meaningful protection from missile attack. This failure undermines the fundamental compact between the citizen and the state, whereby the former gives up some rights and privileges in exchange for security.

The present policy of vulnerability contains a second moral contradiction: Although our government professes to respect human life, it relies on a retaliatory strategy that threatens millions of innocent lives. Imagine if North Korea fired a missile at Los Angeles. If this missile were tipped with a nuclear bomb, deadly biological agent, or chemical weapon, it could inflict hundreds of thousands, perhaps even

> The moral rationale President Reagan articulated in 1983 for developing defenses remains true today. National missile defense is about saving lives and protecting our country.

millions, of casualties. Considering the scale of destruction, the President would have to choose retaliation, which would be likely to result in the deaths of hundreds of thousands (or more) of North Korean civilians—or American capitulation. Neither outcome would be strategically or morally desirable. The ability to intercept incoming missiles would present a morally sound alternative between these two extremes.

Both contradictions are indefensible, considering the availability of technologies that we could deploy to protect our country. As President Reagan asked in his 1983 speech establishing the SDI, "Wouldn't it be better to save lives than to avenge them?" If the moral contradictions in U.S. policy are left unresolved, we risk paying for them with our lives, treasure, and sacred honor.

STRIKING FIRST IS IMMORAL

Attacking enemy missiles in their silos is an alternative to building a defensive shield or relying on retaliatory threats. Yet preemption is not part of our political tradition—and for good reason. Aggressor states like Imperial Japan and Nazi Germany have used this rationale to pursue their dreams of territorial conquest. It would cost us dearly—in moral, political, and strategic terms—if we adopted this posture.[4]

Clearly, a defensive system designed to intercept hostile missiles would be preferable to striking first. It would end our vulnerability without threatening anyone else. If the Department of Defense emphasized preemptive options, other states probably would be encouraged to develop similar weapons and adopt hair-trigger postures. The result—an increased risk of war—would be predictable and unwelcome. Yet, because we lack any protection against hostile missiles, the pressure to adopt such extreme measures like preemption will increase.

The moral rationale President Reagan articulated in 1983 for developing defenses remains true today. National missile defense is about saving lives and protecting our country. That is the reason a defensive system capable of protecting all Americans is morally preferable to deterrence based on the threat of retaliation or any preemptive option.

VULNERABILITY UNDERMINES AMERICA'S LEADERSHIP

Building a national missile defense also would help to preserve our status as a superpower. America has been a positive force for freedom and democratic principles since gaining its independence in 1776. Yet our ability to promote freedom abroad will suffer if we remain defenseless against missile attack. Bereft of any protection, we will leave ourselves open to political coercion, perhaps even nuclear blackmail. Remember the 1991 Persian Gulf War? President George Bush's response to the invasion of Kuwait by Iraq almost certainly would have been different had Saddam Hussein possessed missiles capable of striking the United States.[5]

Or remember when President Reagan ordered the military strike on Libya in 1986 in response to its terrorist attacks on American service personnel? Afterward, Libyan leader Muammar Qadhafi told his followers,

> If they know that you have a deterrent force capable of hitting the United States, they would not be able to hit you. If we had possessed a deterrent—missiles that could reach New York—we would have hit it at the same moment. Consequently, we should build this force so that they and others will no longer think about an attack.[6]

The sad fact is that Colonel Qadhafi probably was right in his assessment. President Reagan—or any other President, for that matter—would have been far less likely to retaliate if a Third World despot like Colonel Qadhafi had been capable of threatening

American cities with ballistic missiles.

More powerful states have recognized that our vulnerability to missile attack at home will restrict our ability to protect vital security interests abroad. In 1996, a senior Chinese official asserted that his government did not worry about America's defending Taiwan because "American leaders care more about Los Angeles than they do about Taiwan."[7]

Our continued vulnerability also would hurt us if an aggressive dictator decided to invade one of our friends or allies. Deploying troops and supplies overseas takes time and effort. It took us six months to build up forces in the Persian Gulf prior to launching Operation Desert Storm. Major staging areas in our country—ports, depots, military bases, and airfields—would be obvious missile targets for an enemy aiming, literally and figuratively, to prevent us from responding to international crises.

DEFENSIVE TECHNOLOGIES HAVE ADVANCED DRAMATICALLY

During the Cold War, we had little choice but to rely on our stockpile of nuclear weapons and the threat of retaliation to dissuade Soviet aggression. At that time, the technologies available to intercept hostile missiles were primitive. Today, however, dramatic progress in technology gives our leaders more choices; we no longer must remain resigned to relying on retaliatory threats to dissuade aggression. Successful missile intercept tests already have shown that we have the potential to develop an effective national missile defense against ballistic missiles launched by rogue states.[8] We have ships that could be equipped with missile interceptors and deployed around the globe. We have satellite technology that would allow us to deploy space-based sensors and interceptors. The refusal of some elected leaders to take missile defense seriously and fund the development and deployment of a missile defense system is itself a moral failing.

ENDING THE FATALISM OF VULNERABILITY

Before World War II, Prime Minister Stanley Baldwin asserted,

> I think it is well for the man in the street to realize that there is no power on earth which can protect him from being bombed. Whatever people may tell him, the bomber will always get through.[9]

Fortunately for Great Britain, not everybody believed Mr. Baldwin. Thanks to the tireless efforts of Winston Churchill and others, Britain built a network of radars and fighter bases to protect the island from German bombers. Their foresight prevented a German cross-channel invasion in World War II.

Today, there are those who also would argue, in effect, that the "missile always will get through." But their perspective reflects a political bias, not an objective technological assessment. Dramatic technological advances in recent years have made building a protective shield both practical and affordable, as a detailed study by a team of experts commissioned by The Heritage Foundation makes clear.[10]

Some critics also claim that protecting ourselves against missile attacks is futile because such a system never could be 100-percent effective. In other words, they reject the idea that *some* protection is better than *no* protection against missiles. That is peculiar logic because even an imperfect defense would save millions of lives in the event of a missile attack.

No weapon system ever has performed perfectly during its testing and development phase. In fact, testing is designed to discover design flaws and work out any bugs before deployment. As President Reagan rightly anticipated in his SDI speech, "There will be failures and setbacks, just as there will be successes and breakthroughs."[11]

If perfection were the standard to assess military programs, we never would deploy any weapon system. The good news is that a leak-proof shield is not necessary to dissuade aggression. A potential adversary plotting a missile attack against us would face tremendous uncertainties even confronted with a less-than-perfect defense.

Imagine if you were a foreign dictator scheming to attack the United States using ballistic missiles. Before attacking, your military leaders could not tell you how many missiles would get through the defenses or even what targets they would hit. Such unknowns as these strengthen deterrence; in other words, a system designed to intercept hostile missiles need not be perfect to dissuade aggression.

Our elected leaders must get beyond the fatalism of vulnerability. They must act to end the morally bankrupt policy of leaving American citizens naked to missile attack. As former Secretary of State Henry Kissinger asserts,

> It is reckless to stake the survival of a society on its vulnerability or on genocidal retaliation—even against an accidental launch. National and theater missile defense must become a higher national priority.[12]

NOTES

1   President Ronald Reagan, *Address to the Nation on National Security,* March 23, 1983.

2   *Ibid.*

3   "Do We Need a Missile Defense System?" *The Washington Times,* May 14, 1996, p. A15.

4   Although preemption is undesirable for the reasons stated above, it nevertheless would be unwise to disclaim it as an option categorically for the simple reason that leaving our adversaries guessing may have some deterrent value.

5   Iraq's use of Scud missiles during the Persian Gulf War also demonstrated the vulnerability of U.S. troops to short-range missiles. In February 1991, the attack on a U.S. troop barracks in Saudi Arabia killed 28 and wounded 100. Significantly, there is evidence of Iraqi efforts to reconstitute the country's missile programs. See R. Jeffrey Smith, "Iraq Buying Missile Parts Covertly; Officials Say Effort Violates Trade Ban," *The Washington Post,* October 14, 1995, p. A1.

6   Speech by Muammar Qadhafi at a meeting of students of the Higher Institute for Applied Social Studies at the Great al-Faith University, April 18, 1990,

Tripoli Television Service, April 19, 1990 (translated in Foreign Broadcast Information Service, *Daily Report: Near East & South Asia,* FBIS-NES-90-078, April 23, 1990, p. 8).

[7] Bill Gertz, "General Who Threatened L.A. Tours U.S. on Chinese Mission; Other in Military Delegation Sold Arms, Missiles Abroad," *The Washington Times,* December 18, 1996, p. A6.

[8] For a chart that identifies successful missile intercept tests, see "HTK Success Amidst HTK-Interceptor Failure," Ballistic Missile Defense Office *Fact Sheet,* March 1999.

[9] Former Prime Minister Stanley Baldwin, in an address before the House of Commons on November 10, 1932, as quoted by former Representative Jim Courter (R-NJ) in "Sir Winston's Wisdom and SDI," *The Washington Times,* January 24, 1986, p. D1.

[10] *Defending America: A Plan to Meet the Urgent Missile Threat,* Report by The Heritage Foundation's Commission on Missile Defense (Washington, D.C.: The Heritage Foundation, 1999).

[11] Reagan, *Address to the Nation on National Security.*

[12] Henry Kissinger, "India and Pakistan: After the Explosion," *The Washington Post,* June 9, 1998, p. A15.

4

BLUEPRINT FOR DEFENDING AMERICA: FIRST FROM THE SEA, THEN FROM SPACE

The most expeditious, least expensive way to provide an effective defense against ballistic missiles is to deploy sea-based defenses first, followed by space-based defenses.

— The Heritage Foundation's Commission on Missile Defense, 1999[1]

In the 1980s, critics ridiculed the Strategic Defense Initiative (SDI) for exploring technologies capable of intercepting hostile missiles. They called this effort "Star Wars" and claimed it was too expensive, too provocative, and too risky. Their relentless criticism exacted a heavy toll. Because of congressional cutbacks, the SDI never advanced beyond the research and limited testing stages.

The money invested in the SDI has not been wasted, however. We know that the mere prospect of deploying a protective shield against missiles hastened the Soviet Union's demise, as evidenced by statements of former senior Soviet leaders. For example, Vladimir

Lukin, Russia's former Ambassador to the United States and now Chairman of the State Duma (Parliament) Foreign Affairs Committee, estimates that the SDI hastened the end of the Cold War by at least five years.[2] The Soviets knew they could not possibly compete with our impressive technological advantages.

More important, President Ronald Reagan's program laid the groundwork for the deployment of a national system that is capable of protecting Americans against hostile missile attack. Thanks to the momentum established by the SDI, research efforts have harvested a range of technologies that, if integrated inside a meaningful system, will afford all Americans protection against the threat of missile attack by rogue states.

THE ELEMENTS OF AN EFFECTIVE MISSILE DEFENSE SYSTEM

A national missile defense would have three main components: sensors, interceptors, and a command-and-control system. Take a closer look at each of these elements to see how they would work together to protect you and your family against enemy missiles.

Chart 4-1 illustrates the necessary elements of an effective, and affordable, missile defense system designed to provide

Chart 4.1

Basic Missile Defense Elements

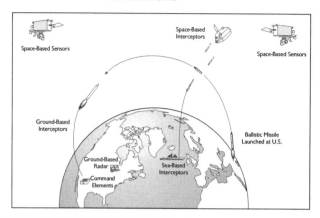

layered protection. These elements include:

- **Sensors.** An effective and affordable
  missile defense system would depend on
  information received from sensors that
  can detect enemy missile launches
  immediately after launch and track their
  trajectory. The sensors should be capable
  of discriminating between real and decoy
  warheads. Space-based sensors would
  offer the earliest possible detection of a
  missile launch and would relay the
  information to interceptors within
  seconds. An effective national missile
  defense system also would incorporate a
  network of land-, air- and sea-based
  sensors.

- **Interceptors.** To destroy enemy missiles before they reached their intended targets, the missile defense system would need interceptors. There are two basic varieties of interceptors: kinetic weapons and lasers. Kinetic weapons would use small projectiles to interdict and destroy incoming missiles on impact; lasers would project a beam of energy that achieved the same result. Interceptors could be air-, space-, sea- or ground-based. A national defense system should be capable of intercepting a hostile missile anywhere along its flight trajectory—the earlier, though, the better.

  The best time to intercept an enemy missile is shortly after takeoff during its so-called boost phase. At this stage, the missile is easiest to detect because it emits a large exhaust plume. The most difficult point—and therefore the least desirable time to intercept—is shortly before impact, during the missile's "terminal phase." At this stage, the incoming warhead is moving at great speed, and intercepting it within the earth's atmosphere would result in deadly fallout over our country.

- **A command-and-control system.** Managing this system would require a command-and-control network that would allow different parts of the system to communicate with one another and relay information in a timely and accurate manner. It should have some built-in redundancy; otherwise, an enemy could succeed in "decapitating" the entire system by knocking out a single component.

Putting the Elements Together

Thanks to the money already spent on researching missile defense technologies, an integrated system composed of sensors, interceptors, and a command-and-control network would be both practical and affordable. In 1998, The Heritage Foundation commissioned a panel of defense experts to examine the most effective and affordable architecture for such a system.[3] Chaired by Ambassador Henry Cooper, the former Director of the Strategic Defense Initiative Organization and Chief U.S. Negotiator to the Geneva Defense and Space Talks with the Soviet Union, the Commission on Missile Defense included such experts as Fred Iklé, former Undersecretary of Defense for Policy and Director of the Arms Control and Disarmament Agency.

The Commission on Missile Defense issued its conclusions in March 1999. It recommended a defense architecture that capitalizes on the investment the military has made already in the U.S. Navy's Aegis system. The Navy has 22 Aegis cruisers capable of defending themselves against air and cruise missile attacks. With a modest investment, this system could be upgraded to intercept hostile missiles fired at American citizens. This should be Washington's first priority. Following this step, the Department of Defense should develop and deploy space-based interceptors to provide another layer of protection.

It should be noted that the Commission's recommendation to build a sea- and space-based system contrasts sharply with the ground-based proposal of the Clinton Administration.[4] That scheme would be more costly and would fail to provide any defense-in-depth.

How Would This Impact Arms-Reduction Efforts?

Critics often charge that building a national missile defense would prompt a new arms race. This charge is yet another scare tactic propagated by diehard opponents of national missile defense. Because of dramatic technological advances, deploying a national missile defense would not require the United States to build any additional nuclear weapons. The defensive technologies under consideration are non-nuclear. Asserting that such a system somehow would be "offensive" is akin to arguing that a police officer's donning a bulletproof vest is "provocative" to criminals.

Further, deployment of a national missile defense would not ruin arms control prospects with Russia, as opponents often claim. In fact, the deployment of a national missile defense would be likely to enhance the prospects for substantive nuclear arms reductions without compromising our national security. Effective defenses devalue offensive missiles, making meaningful reductions possible. In this vein, it is worth recalling that President Reagan made significant progress toward reducing the level of offensive nuclear weapons at the same time that he championed strategic defenses.[5]

> Thanks to the money already spent on researching missile defense technologies, an integrated system composed of sensors, interceptors, and a command-and-control network is both practical and affordable.

The decision to deploy an effective national missile defense would require us to move beyond the 1972 Anti-Ballistic Missile Treaty. Because it no longer is legally binding, this Cold War fossil should not be an impediment to deploying a defensive system. This conclusion is detailed in a comprehensive legal study prepared for The Heritage Foundation by the law firm Hunton & Williams in 1998;[6] and it has been endorsed by numerous legal and foreign policy experts, including former Secretary of State Henry Kissinger, who was National Security Adviser to the President during the negotiation of the original treaty.

What About the Cost?

Critics had claimed that the SDI would bust the budget. One estimate, endlessly repeated by the media in the 1980s, pegged the cost of protecting America from missile assault at $1 trillion.[7]

Today, the projected costs for a system to protect American citizens are measured in the tens of billions of dollars. This may sound like a lot of money, and indeed it is. But this estimate must be placed in a larger context. The United States is the wealthiest country in the world, and the expense of deploying a protective system against hostile missiles would be stretched over several years. Considering current budget protections, it is unlikely any such system would consume more than 2 percent of defense expenditures during that time period. That would be a small price to pay to ensure our safety, especially when you consider the cost of a nuclear, biological, or chemical weapon hitting an American city.

Heritage's Commission on Missile Defense concludes that "within four years, and for less than $8 billion, the United States could have an effective and affordable global missile defense system." This is less than the country spends on air traffic control in two years.[8]

Why Are Cost Estimates Smaller Now?

There are two reasons that the cost estimates for a deploying a system to protect us against hostile missiles have dropped considerably in recent years. First, opponents of the SDI wildly exaggerated some of the initial cost estimates. Second, technology has advanced much faster than anticipated. Computer chips are becoming far more sophisticated and cheaper every year.

Recent advances in computer capabilities favor defensive systems because ballistic missiles rely on mature technologies. The Scud missile Saddam Hussein used on Iraq's behalf in the 1990–1991 Persian Gulf War is essentially an updated version of the V-2 missile the Nazis used during World War II. Our technological superiority also would give us a comparative advantage over other states that may seek countermeasures, such as decoy warheads.

What About Countermeasures?

Opponents of national missile defense also argue that any system could be overwhelmed by cheap countermeasures, such as decoy warheads, or that a space-based anti-missile system would itself be vulnerable to attack. Some claim that we would risk building a "Maginot Line" in the sky—a reference to an elaborate series of French fortifications the German *Blitzkrieg* circumvented in World War II.

> Heritage's Commission on Missile Defense concludes that "within four years, and for less than $8 billion, the United States could have an effective and affordable global missile defense system."

Properly designed, a system to protect against hostile missiles should be able to neutralize potential countermeasures. It would have inherent self-defense capabilities against such attacks. For example, space-based sensors could be protected against countermeasures by making them maneuverable or by coating them with special materials to help them to evade detection.[9]

A robust system to protect against enemy missiles should include several layers. The first and most important layer would seek to intercept missiles in their boost phase. Such a system would destroy an enemy's ability to release individual warheads and decoys. This capability would serve as a powerful deterrent because any resultant fallout would land on the aggressor's own territory. If the missile escaped a boost-phase intercept, we still would have additional layers of defenses to shoot it down before it reached our country.

WHAT IS NEEDED NOW

We cannot afford to remain defenseless against hostile missiles. The loss of a single city to a nuclear weapon would claim more civilian victims than all our previous wars combined. Such an attack would dwarf the damage caused by the terrorist strikes on the World Trade Center and the federal building in Oklahoma City. A missile attack would threaten the very existence of America's constitutional system and endanger the freedoms we often take for granted.

If you own a home or automobile, you probably pay for some form of insurance. That is prudent, considering the potential for financial loss in the case of fire, flood, or some other disaster. Fielding a system to defend America against hostile missiles should be considered a form of insurance. It would require paying an annual premium to protect against catastrophic loss.

A missile defense is affordable if we pursue the sea- and space-based defenses outlined here. America is blessed with ample brainpower and technological expertise to build a system that is capable of protecting all Americans. What is lacking is the political will to deploy it.

NOTES

1 *Defending America: A Plan to Meet the Urgent Missile Threat,* Report by The Heritage Foundation's Commission on Missile Defense (Washington, D.C.: The Heritage Foundation, 1999).

2 *Ibid.,* p. 44.

3 *Ibid.*

4 *Ibid.*

5 President Reagan signed the Intermediate-Range Nuclear Forces (INF) Treaty in December 1987, eliminating an entire class of weapons. He also negotiated the Strategic Arms Reduction Treaty (START) I, which, unlike previous arms control agreements, called for the actual reduction of nuclear weapons.

6 David B. Rivkin, Jr., Lee A. Casey, and Darin R. Bartram, "The Collapse of the Soviet Union and the End of the 1972

Anti-Ballistic Missile Treaty: A Memorandum of Law," The Heritage Foundation, June 15, 1998.

[7] For example, see Mary McGrory, "A Question of Infallibility?" *The Washington Post,* October 16, 1986, p. A2.

[8] Based on fiscal year 1998 actual expenditures. From U.S. Department of Transportation, "Federal Aviation Administration Budget in Brief, Fiscal Year 2000," 1999.

[9] We already have applied stealth technology successfully to some of our aircraft, including the F-117 and B-2.

5

NO TIME TO LOSE: WHAT THE ADMINISTRATION, CONGRESS, AND CITIZENS MUST DO

I cannot imagine what an American President would say to the American public if there was [a missile] attack and he had done nothing to prevent it.
— Former Secretary of State Henry Kissinger, 1999[1]

The decision to build a national missile defense should have been made years ago. That lost time never can be recovered; the important point now is not to lose any more time. It is not too late to deploy effective defenses to protect you and your family here at home, our troops overseas, and our allies who may be threatened, but there is no virtue in tempting fate by waiting any longer. The alarming proliferation of these deadly weapons, especially to the dictators of rogue states, is abundantly clear.[2] If an American city is destroyed by an enemy missile attack, it will not be for lack of warning.

SURVIVING THE AGE OF PROLIFERATION

We live in the age of proliferation—an unpleasant fact of life that puts our national security at risk. The Clinton Administration, as well as future presidential administrations, should exert intense diplomatic and economic pressure to discourage proliferation.[3] But we should not deceive ourselves that such efforts alone will suffice to protect us. Unconstrained by legal or moral constraints, Third World states continue to work feverishly to develop ballistic missiles. Clearly, states like North Korea and Iran hope to exploit our vulnerability. We should procrastinate no longer to defend ourselves against missile attack.

The Choice

Americans face basic choices that will determine how we both live as a people and relate with the rest of the world. If diehard opponents of a national missile defense have their way, we will remain vulnerable to the most destructive weapons ever invented. If the Clinton Administration eventually follows through with its plan, it will deploy a costly and ineffective ground-based system. In both cases, future dictators will have, at their whim, the capacity to threaten the lives of millions of Americans with long-range missiles; the President will be forced to think twice about honoring our security agreements abroad because of our vulnerability at home; and danger of accidental or unauthorized missile launches will grow over time.

There is, thankfully, another path we can take. The 21st century can be one of unparalleled peace and prosperity—for you as a citizen and for the United States as a whole—but only if we take prudent measures to protect ourselves. The most important thing we can do is build a robust, sea- and space-based defense that exploits our technological advantages. Rogue states still will cause trouble and create mischief with their neighbors, but at least they will not have the potential to threaten millions of Americans with their deadly missiles.

WHAT THE ADMINISTRATION SHOULD DO

After years of downplaying the threat of missile proliferation, the Clinton Administration finally admits it is real and growing. This is a welcome, although belated, admission. Now, we must ask the Administration to take the next logical step and commit the United States to deploying an effective national missile defense.

The President must act. After all, he bears the ultimate responsibility for ensuring that America is protected against foreign threats. The Clinton Administration's decision to put off a deployment decision until June 2000 is a policy of procrastination. It should be shelved. We should focus on the missile threat today, not some arbitrary calendar date in the future.

President Clinton should declare his firm commitment to deploy an effective missile defense system as soon as technologically possible. This should be accompanied by the clear declaration that the 1972 Anti-Ballistic Missile (ABM) Treaty is legally dead. These actions should not be put off until next year, next month, or even next week. These actions should be taken today.

> Congress must pressure the Clinton Administration to make a deployment decision sooner rather than later.

We never can be sure exactly when the next natural disaster will strike. Despite our best efforts to forecast the weather, nature is full of nasty surprises. In like manner, it is not always possible to know when, where, or in what manner an adversary will attack. In 1941, we failed to anticipate Japan's attack on Pearl Harbor; in 1950, we failed to foresee

North Korea's invasion of South Korea; and in 1990, we failed to predict Saddam Hussein's invasion of Kuwait.

What will be our next big surprise? The harsh reality is that we may not know ahead of time when an enemy will decide to unleash missiles, or what targets he will select. Prudence dictates that the President decide to deploy defenses sooner rather than later.

WHAT CONGRESS SHOULD DO

Congress needs to pressure the Clinton Administration to make a deployment decision. Toward this end, it should hold hearings to examine the costs and risks associated with the Administration's policy of procrastination. Congress should consider legislation to ensure that testing is not constrained by the defunct ABM Treaty. And it should force the Administration to explain the reason it is allowing Russia, with its opposition to U.S. missile defense efforts, to exercise, in effect, a veto power over our ability to protect against Third World missile threats.

Equally important, Congress should press the Clinton Administration to explain its preference for a ground-based system when less costly and more effective defensive technologies are available. Considering the urgency of the threat, logic dictates that our country commit to building the best possible defense. This requires a broader set of testing than currently is planned by the Administration.

Congress must pressure the Clinton Administration to make a deployment decision sooner rather than later. It should exercise its oversight responsibilities to ensure that the management of the national missile defense program be streamlined so that red tape does not prevent rapid development, testing, and deployment. Once a deployment decision is made, Congress must allocate sufficient funds to provide the American people with the best possible defense against hostile missiles.

As with any military program, the deployment of a national missile defense will require periodic improvements. Congress has a vital role to play here as well. A sustained congressional effort will be required to ensure all Americans are properly protected throughout the 21st century.

WHAT CITIZENS SHOULD DO

Sometimes our elected leaders need a little shove to get them to act. This is the reason that concerned citizens like yourself have an important role to play in this debate.

Will we be remembered for squandering away all advantages wrought by the end of the Cold War? Or will we marshal the political will necessary to provide for our security? These are not idle questions. History will judge our generation by what we do—and by what we leave undone. If we fail to protect ourselves, we will jeopardize our constitutional freedoms and those of all future generations of Americans.

Citizens have every right to expect their government to protect them from security threats, whether they originate from domestic extremists or rogue states developing long-range missiles. As Winston Churchill stated,

> The exertions which a nation is prepared to make to protect its individual representatives or citizens from outrage is one of the truest measures of its greatness as an organized state.[4]

By failing to protect its citizens, Washington is abrogating its responsibility. No government can endure long without fulfilling its constitutional obligation to defend its citizens.

The debate over national missile defense is too important to be left to Washington insiders. You need to make your voice heard as a concerned and well-informed citizen. By reading this book, you already are demonstrating your interest. Now that you know the main arguments in the missile defense debate, you can help to make sure America does not remain at risk.

Grassroots Activism

To assist the growing number of citizens who support the deployment of a national missile defense, you can:

- **Form** a national missile defense discussion group. Meet on a monthly basis and educate your fellow citizens about this issue;

- **Read** the unclassified Executive Summary of the Rumsfeld Commission Report on the proliferation of ballistic missiles on the Internet at *http://www.fas.org/irp/threat/bm-threat.htm;*

- **Deepen** your understanding of missile defense issues by visiting Internet sites on missile defense, such as Heritage's site at *http://www.heritage.org,* the Center for Security Policy's at *http://www.security-policy.org,* and High Frontier's at *http://www.erols.com/hifront.* Download articles and policy papers to distribute among your friends, family, and community groups;

- **Contact** your representatives in Congress and find out their positions on national missile defense and their voting records;

- **Learn** more about the candidates for the Presidency in 2000 and where they stand on missile defense; and
- **Keep** abreast of the growing Third World missile threat by reading articles in newspapers, magazines, and journals.

WE THE PEOPLE

The threat of ballistic missile attack is not a Hollywood fantasy or a plot in a Tom Clancy novel; it is a harsh reality that cannot be wished away. Last August, North Korea tested a missile that probably has the ability to strike the outer reaches of Hawaii and Alaska. North Korea is working overtime on an even more advanced missile that could hit the continental United States. Coming from a regime whose people are starving to death, these efforts reflect a desperate desire to threaten our country and our allies.

North Korea's is not the only dictatorship we have to worry about. Iran, Libya, and Syria are among the nearly two dozen states hoping to gain political and military leverage by developing ballistic missiles. And we should not ignore Russia and China, two powerful states with uncertain political futures that already have long-range missiles capable of reaching our cities.

In a sense, we have come full circle in our history to a point at which the physical security of all Americans is again at risk. Our Founding Fathers were gravely concerned that foreign predators would exploit our weaknesses as a fledgling republic. Although we now are a mature republic, we face many menacing security challenges. So long as we remain a free people, we retain the ability to shape our own destiny. The choice, then, is ours.

Our system of government is based on the consent of the governed. That is the reason our Constitution begins with the phrase "We the People." Sometimes, when the country's leaders fail to take the right course of action, the people must lead. If we remain passive, the forces of inertia will triumph and the decision to deploy a national missile defense may be postponed indefinitely. If the Clinton Administration eventually makes the decision to field a defense against missile attack, there is no guarantee that it will commit to building the best possible defense—one unencumbered by a defunct ABM Treaty. On the other hand, if we make our voices heard, we are likely to get the protection we deserve.

NOTES

[1]   Editorial, "Some Future Kosovo," *The Wall Street Journal,* March 29, 1999.

[2]   See generally *The Proliferation Primer, A Majority Report of the Subcommittee on International Security, Proliferation, and Federal Services,* Committee on Governmental Affairs, U.S. Senate, 105th Cong., January 1998.

[3]   For an analysis of the ways in which the Clinton Administration exacerbated the proliferation problem with respect to China, see Edward Timperlake and William Triplett II, *Year of the Rat: How Bill Clinton Compromised U.S. Security for Chinese Cash* (Washington, D.C.: Regnery Publishing, 1998).

[4]   Winston S. Churchill, "Paper for the War Cabinet," September 3, 1918.

GLOSSARY

ABM Treaty (Anti-Ballistic Missile Treaty)—
A treaty signed by the United States and the
Soviet Union in 1972 that forbade either
superpower from developing a nationwide
defense against missiles. Many international
legal scholars now assert that America's
obligation to this treaty ended when the
Soviet Union dissolved in 1991 because
neither Russia nor any combination of
former Soviet states can fulfill its original
purposes.

accidental launch—A launch that could
occur if a state mistakenly believed it was
under attack. This also could happen because
of a computer malfunction or sheer
incompetence on the part of a radar
operator. Thinking its own missiles might be
destroyed on the ground, an adversary might
conclude it is better to "use them or lose
them." See also *unauthorized launch*.

architecture—The organizing framework that
melds together specific components of a
national missile defense. These include
sensors to track missiles and warheads,
interceptors to destroy them, and a
command-and-control process to manage the

entire system. The Clinton Administration's proposed architecture for a national missile defense calls for ground-based interceptors positioned at only one or two sites. A more effective and less costly architecture for missile defense would use both sea- and space-based interceptors, as detailed in The Heritage Foundation's 1999 report, *Defending America: A Plan to Meet the Urgent Missile Threat.*

arms control—Legal efforts aimed at controlling the research, development, and deployment of weapons. Such measures can be quantitative (placing limits on the number of weapons deployed) or qualitative (restricting technological developments). The ABM Treaty puts quantitative and qualitative restrictions on America's ability to deploy a national missile defense. The United States signed numerous arms control treaties with the Soviet Union during the Cold War. Arms control agreements are desirable insofar as they contribute to U.S. security, but they should not be pursued for their own sake.

ballistic missile—Unlike cruise missiles, ballistic missiles are propelled by rocket engines outside the earth's atmosphere. They travel through space before reentering the atmosphere and rely on gravity to reach their intended targets. By contrast, a cruise missile works like an unpiloted airplane; its engine draws oxygen for combustion as it flies through the atmosphere.

biological weapons—Pound for pound, the most lethal substances known to mankind. They can be disseminated by various means of delivery, including aerial bombs, spray tanks, and missile warheads. Such agents include anthrax, smallpox, and the plague.

BMDO (Ballistic Missile Defense Organization)—An agency of the U.S. Department of Defense that manages research programs examining the feasibility of eliminating the threat posed by ballistic missiles of all ranges. It is the successor to the Strategic Defense Initiative Organization (SDIO).

boost phase—The part of the rocket's flight that occurs immediately after liftoff. During this phase, ballistic missiles are propelled by their engines. For an intercontinental ballistic missile (ICBM), this phase usually lasts from three to five minutes. The boost phase ends once the missile no longer relies on its engines for flight, a stage that typically occurs when the missile reaches an altitude of approximately 200 kilometers (or 124 miles).

chemical weapons—Highly toxic substances designed to kill or incapacitate people. Chemical weapons include choking, blood, and nerve agents. They can be disseminated by various means of delivery, including aerial bombs, artillery shells, and missile warheads.

decoys—Devices that simulate a real warhead. Their presence may make it difficult for an interceptor to find and destroy the actual warheads. A national missile defense system should be capable of intercepting all hostile missiles in their boost phase—before the decoys and warhead are deployed. See also *boost phase.*

deployment—The actual construction of a national missile defense, as opposed to research and development. President Bill Clinton has stated that he will not commit to making a deployment decision until June 2000.

deterrence—The ability to dissuade aggression. Deterrence has both a physical and rational dimension. The physical component consists of having the military capability to inflict unacceptable damage via retaliatory strikes. The rational component involves convincing your enemy that such a response is a certainty. Both elements must be present for deterrence to work. History, however, shows that foreign despots do not always base their decisions on rational calculations.

delivery system—The means by which warheads reach their targets. Delivery systems include bombers, cruise missiles, and ballistic missiles.

GPALS (Global Protection Against Limited Strikes)—A program announced by President George Bush in his January 1991 State of the Union address. He directed that the Strategic Defense Initiative (SDI) be "refocused on providing protection from limited ballistic missile strikes—whatever their source." This reorientation was appropriate because the threat no longer involved a massive attack from the Soviet Union. GPALS was designed to protect us against Third World ballistic missile threats and the possibility of accidental or unauthorized launches by Russia or China. President Bush's plan called for deployment to begin in 1996. President Clinton canceled GPALS in 1993, thus delaying any deployment decision for many years.

ICBMs (intercontinental ballistic missiles)—Missiles that can cross oceans or entire continents to hit intended targets. Their ranges are greater than 5,500 kilometers (or 3,417 miles). The term *ICBM* is used only for land-based systems. In its report on the ballistic missile threat, the Rumsfeld Commission cautions that an enemy does not have to possess ICBMs to attack an American city; instead, he might mount shorter-range missiles on delivery systems, such as a tramp steamer, that can be positioned off our coastline.

interceptors—Weapons that destroy hostile ballistic missiles after launch. Two types of interceptors are under development: kinetic-energy weapons, which include non-explosive projectiles, and lasers, which use beams of directed energy. See also *kinetic weapons* and *lasers.*

IRBMs (intermediate-range ballistic missiles)—Ballistic missiles with ranges from 1,000 to 5,500 kilometers (or 621 to 3,417 miles).

kinetic weapons—Non-explosive projectiles that move at high speeds to destroy targets. Kinetic weapons also may carry homing sensors to improve their accuracy.

laser—A device that focuses a narrow, intense beam of light that destroys targets by heating, melting, or vaporizing them.

MAD (mutual assured destruction)—A Cold War dogma that the United States and the Soviet Union would find virtue in their respective vulnerability: Neither side would be tempted to launch a nuclear strike because the other power would unleash a devastating riposte. In effect, MAD was a mutual suicide pact that was given legal expression in the 1972 ABM Treaty forbidding either superpower from building national missile defense systems. See also *ABM Treaty*.

megaton—A measure of explosive power; 1 megaton is equivalent to 1 million tons of TNT. The nuclear bomb dropped on Hiroshima unleashed an explosion that was equivalent to 15,000 tons of TNT. Both the United States and Russia have multi-megaton warheads.

national missile defense—A generic term to describe a system capable of protecting a country from missile attack The Clinton Administration favors a ground-based missile defense system. A team of experts commissioned by The Heritage Foundation has concluded that this approach would be less effective and more costly than a system using on sea- and space-based platforms.

nuclear fallout—Radioactive debris from a nuclear disaster. The size and intensity of the fallout depends on the weapon used, the altitude at which it is detonated, and atmospheric conditions, including prevailing winds.

proliferation—The spread of weapons technology and know-how to other countries. The most serious forms of proliferation involve nuclear, biological, and chemical weapons. In November 1994, President Clinton signed Executive Order No. 12938, which found that the "proliferation of nuclear, biological, and chemical weapons ("weapons of mass destruction") and of the means of delivering such weapons, constitutes an unusual and extraordinary threat to the national security, foreign policy, and economy of the United States." He "declare[d] a national emergency to deal with that threat." Despite his executive order, the President has yet to commit to deploying a national missile defense.

rogue states—Countries that do not respect international norms of civilized behavior; instead, they sow seeds of disorder by supporting international terrorism and threatening other countries. Several rogue states, including Iran and North Korea, are seeking long-range missiles capable of reaching American cities. Such states are dangerous because their leaders are unpredictable; threats of retaliation may not dissuade them from attacking.

Rumsfeld Commission—A congressionally mandated bipartisan commission that examined the threat of ballistic missile attack on the United States. On July 15, 1998, the commission rejected a 1995 U.S. National Intelligence Estimate that the America would face no direct ballistic missile threat before 2010. The commission asserted that the "threat to the U.S. posed by these emerging capabilities is broader, more mature and evolving more rapidly than has been reported in estimates and reports by the Intelligence Community." The commission's report provides Congress with a much-needed wakeup call about the growing threat of missile proliferation.

Scud—A short-range ballistic missile that can reach 180 to 550 kilometers (or 111 to 342 miles), depending on the variant. Iraq's Saddam Hussein terrorized Israel and Saudi Arabia with Scud missile attacks during the Persian Gulf War in 1991. A Scud attack on a U.S. barracks in Saudi Arabia killed more Americans than any other incident in that conflict. The Rumsfeld Commission pointed out that states capable of building Scud missiles have the inherent potential to develop missiles with much longer ranges.

SDI (Strategic Defense Initiative)—A program announced by President Ronald Reagan in his Address to the Nation on National Security on March 23, 1983, when he called "upon the scientific community in our country, those who gave us nuclear weapons, to turn their great talents now to the cause of mankind and world peace, to give us the means of rendering these nuclear weapons impotent and obsolete." He thus challenged the conventional wisdom that deterrence was best served by preserving a mutual suicide pact with the Soviet Union. President Reagan believed this posture was immoral and costly. Congressional opposition prevented the SDI from moving beyond its research and development phase. The program nevertheless helped win the Cold War by convincing Soviet leaders they could not possibly compete with our advanced technologies. It also laid the groundwork for technologies America can use today to begin deploying cost-effective defenses against Third World missile threats.

strategic stability—A mantra often invoked by the Clinton Administration to justify its support of the 1972 ABM Treaty, which perpetuates our vulnerability to missile attack. The real test of stability is whether U.S. defense policies will make an enemy missile attack more or less likely. See also *ABM Treaty.*

theater missile defense—Systems capable of protecting geographic areas outside the United States against enemy missiles. These defenses may be deployed to protect U.S. troops, allied forces, or civilian populations.

unauthorized launch—A launch that could occur if a rogue leader were to seize control of a country's ballistic missiles. In our country, ballistic missiles are subject to tight political control; the military cannot launch missiles without the President's authorization. Not every country has a stable political system or long tradition of civilian control over the military, however.

warheads—Destructive payloads carried by missiles. Warheads may contain nuclear, biological, chemical, or conventional munitions. Some ballistic missiles also may carry dummy warheads, or decoys, to confuse interceptors. That is the reason it is vital to have a defense system capable of shooting down hostile missiles in their boost phase. See also *boost phase.*

weapons of mass destruction—A generic term that refers to nuclear, biological, or chemical, munitions capable of destroying life and property on a massive scale. Ballistic missiles can be tipped with warheads that carry weapons of mass destruction.

ANSWERING FREQUENTLY ASKED QUESTIONS ABOUT MISSILE DEFENSE

Q. What should our national missile defense system look like?

A. An effective national missile defense that will protect Americans here at home, our troops stationed overseas, and our allies would require three elements: (1) sensors capable of detecting enemy missile launches and tracking their trajectory through space; (2) interceptors capable of destroying the missiles in flight and discriminating between real and dummy warheads; and (3) an integrated command-and-control network capable of managing the entire system. Thanks to the money already spent on researching missile defense technologies, America is capable of building such a system that is both practical and affordable.

Q. Wouldn't the deployment of a national missile defense bust the budget?

A. No. The best estimates indicate that developing a system capable of protecting our territory is readily affordable. The Heritage Foundation's Commission on

Missile Defense projects we can develop and deploy an effective system in four years for less than $8 billion. By comparison, we currently spend $6 billion a year on our air traffic control systems. The potential costs of failing to protect American lives against hostile missile attack are staggering.

Q. Wouldn't building a national missile defense prompt a new arms race?

A. No. That charge is another scare tactic propagated by opponents of a national missile defense. Because of dramatic technological advances, deploying a national missile defense would not require the United States to build additional nuclear weapons—not even one. The defensive technologies in development are non-nuclear. Asserting that such a defensive system is "offensive" is like arguing that a police officer's bulletproof vest is provocative to criminals. Deployment of a national missile defense would be likely to enhance the prospects for substantive nuclear arms reductions without compromising national security. President Ronald Reagan, for example, made significant progress toward reducing the level of offensive nuclear weapons at the same time as he

championed strategic defenses. He signed
the Intermediate-Range Nuclear Forces
(INF) Treaty in December 1987, which
eliminated an entire class of nuclear
weapons. And he negotiated the Strategic
Arms Reduction Treaty (START) I, which,
unlike previous arms control agreements,
called for the actual reduction of nuclear
weapons.

Q. **Wouldn't deploying a national missile
defense militarize space?**

A. We are one of several countries that
already have satellites in space to help us
to keep a watchful eye on our adversaries.
They provide warning, as happened when
Saddam Hussein mobilized Iraqi tanks
along the border with Kuwait, and allow
us to communicate instantaneously with
our military forces overseas. Opponents
of missile defense who raise this
objection should express outrage instead
about the potential for offensive ballistic
missiles to "militarize" space. Their
silence on this crucial point betrays a bias
against missile defense. Protecting human
life on earth—not empty space—is the
moral imperative.

Q. **Shouldn't we wait for technology to
"mature" before deploying defenses
against enemy missiles?**

A. The Clinton Administration has used this rationale for postponing deployment of a national missile defense. It allows the Administration to appear concerned about the missile threat without actually doing anything to counter it. Imagine if a police chief decided to withhold bulletproof vests from his patrol officers because more technologically advanced vests were in research and development. That chief would not last five minutes in office. Or imagine that your local hospital refused to operate on someone in your family because a more sophisticated scalpel was being developed. You would quickly find another hospital! Yet critics of missile defense embrace this peculiar logic to justify postponing deployment of a national missile shield. It is a convenient excuse for inaction because technology is always maturing. By this reasoning, the time for deployment never will be ripe.

Q. **The United States still has thousands of nuclear weapons. Why isn't the threat of nuclear retaliation enough to deter rogue states from launching missiles at the United States?**

A. Some foreign leaders may not be deterred by the threat of reprisal. It is difficult to fathom the mindset of a leader like North

Korea's Kim Jong-Il, who spends millions of dollars developing ballistic missiles while many men, women, and children in his country starve. A threat to inflict widespread destruction on North Korea may not dissuade Kim from launching a missile against us. A policy of deterrence presumes that heads of foreign government will be deterred by the threat of retaliation. But history has proved that foreign despots do not always behave predictably, as Iraq's Saddam Hussein repeatedly demonstrates.

Q. Would the decision to deploy a national missile defense system undermine arms control, including the 1972 Anti-Ballistic Missile (ABM) Treaty?

A. On the contrary, the decision to move forward with a defensive system is more likely to spur meaningful arms control. The greatest progress in arms control was achieved during the late 1980s and early 1990s, when our leaders appeared most determined to deploy a defensive system. The decision to deploy a robust national missile defense would require us to move beyond the ABM Treaty. This Cold War fossil should not be considered an impediment to deploying a defensive system because it no longer is legally binding. This conclusion, detailed in a comprehensive legal study prepared for The Heritage Foundation by the law firm Hunton & Williams in 1998, has been endorsed by numerous legal and foreign policy experts, including Henry Kissinger, who was National Security Adviser to the President when the original ABM Treaty was negotiated.

Q. **Wouldn't allowing the ABM Treaty to lapse ruin relations with Russia and make the threat worse?**

A. No. U.S.-Russia relations are influenced by many political and economic factors apart from the status of the ABM Treaty. In any event, we already face the danger of accidental or unauthorized missile launches from an increasingly unstable Russia. Revealingly, Russia has opposed Western policy initiatives on many fronts that have nothing to do with the ABM issue, including, for example, the enlargement of the North Atlantic Treaty Organization (NATO). Because Russia's political future remains uncertain, our leaders have the duty to protect us from missile threats from any source.

Q. **Why spend money on protecting ourselves from hostile missiles when terrorists might try to sneak nuclear,**

biological, or chemical weapons into
our country in a suitcase?

A. The possibility of a terrorist strike on our
soil is no reason to leave our country
naked to missile attack. Taking the
missile threat seriously does *not* imply
that the terrorist threat is somehow
unimportant. A homeowner aiming to
deter burglars would not take pains to
lock the doors and deliberately leave
windows wide open. Our country needs
to defend against a full range of lethal
threats, whether they arise from suitcase-
toting terrorists or ballistic missiles
tipped with deadly weapons.

Q. **Considering that there is no such thing
as a perfect defense against hostile
missiles, why build one in the first
place?**

A. The "perfect defense" argument is a red
herring. If perfection were the standard
by which all military programs were
judged, then our country never would be
able to deploy any programs whatsoever.
A perfect defense is not necessary to
dissuade aggression. An enemy
contemplating a missile attack on
America still would face grave
uncertainties even if confronted by, say, a
defense that were effective 75 percent of
the time. The potential attacker could not

be sure how many missiles would get through or what targets they would destroy; such unknowns as these strengthen deterrence. Having the potential to destroy an enemy's missile in the boost phase means its nuclear, biological, or chemical payload would rain down on the aggressor's own country. That is a powerful deterrent. And even if an irrational actor decided to attack our country after all, an imperfect defense clearly would be preferable to no defense whatsoever.

Q. Would a national missile defense be vulnerable to cheap countermeasures, such as decoy warheads?

A. No. A properly designed system should be able to anticipate and neutralize potential countermeasures. For example, a defensive system that could intercept enemy missiles shortly after liftoff would allow their destruction before they could release individual warheads and decoys. By exploiting America's impressive technological advantages, we should be able to deploy a defensive system capable of anticipating and offsetting a wide range of potential countermeasures.

Q. Why is the issue of national missile defense a moral issue?

A. Our government's first duty is to provide for the common defense. A policy that purposely leaves us vulnerable to attack, when technologies capable of protecting us show great promise yet remain underfunded, is immoral. Moreover, if a country attacked us with missiles, the President would have no alternative today but to retaliate—which would be likely to result in the death of millions of innocent lives—or capitulate. Deploying a defensive system to protect us from hostile missiles is a morally sound alternative that lies between these two extremes. As President Reagan asked in his speech establishing the Strategic Defense Initiative in 1983, "Wouldn't be better to save lives than to avenge them?"